Divorce Discourses
A Biblical Dilemma

About the author

Denzil Chetty is currently lecturing Comparative Religions in the School of Religion and Theology at the University of KwaZulu-Natal (UKZN) South Africa. Chetty is currently researching 'Religious Rhetoric and the Myth of Ethnic Conflict — A Case Study of Cultural Conflict in India (Kashmir). He is also serving as the Editorial Assistant for *Alternation,* Journal for the Study of Southern African Literature and Language and is the Managing Editor of *Nidān,* Journal for the Study of Hinduism. In 2003, Chetty was awarded the prestigious title of an Abe Bailey Scholar for his exceptional leadership qualities and his outstanding academic achievements. He is an ordained Minister in the assemblies of God-South Africa and the Director of a non-profitable community organization called Masakhane cc. Skills, Education, Training & Development Centre.

Divorce Discourses

A Biblical Dilemma

Denzil Chetty

CONCEPT PUBLISHING COMPANY, NEW DELHI-110059

Cataloging in Publication Data—DK
Courtesy: D.K. Agencies (P) Ltd. <docinfo@dkagencies.com>

Chetty, Denzil.
Divorce discourses : a Biblical dilemma / Denzil Chetty.
p. cm.
Includes bibliographical references (p.)
Includes index.
ISBN 8180693880

1. Divorce—Religious aspects—Christianity. 2. Bible.—Criticism, interpretation, etc. 3. Israel—Civilization. I. Title.

DDC 261.835 89 22

ISBN : 81-8069-388-0

First Published 2007

Published and Printed by
Ashok Kumar Mittal
Concept Publishing Company
A/15-16, Commercial Block, Mohan Garden,
New Delhi-110059 (India)

Phones : 25351460, 25351794
Fax : 091-11-25357103
Email : publishing@conceptpub.com

To my parents,
Reverend Adrian S. Chetty & Mrs. S. Chetty,
For their inspiration and guidance which
has been my success.

The Abe Bailey Trust for induction into
their prestigious fellowship.
Dr. J. Gibbons & Ian Leach (Canada, Ontario)
for their inspiration and an experience of a lifetime
in the United Kingdom,
And finally to the Abe Bailey Scholars of 2003,
for ever growing friendship in a never ending journey.

REVIEW

The last part of the title of this book – *'Forced to Divorce'* – originated when I mentioned to the author inadvertently the discourse concerning 'forced divorce' during one of our discussions. He, however, without argument took up the challenge and produced an outstanding piece of work. Although, the study deals with the concept of divorce in an academic way by studying the ancient texts, the current challenges of the divorce discourse is also confronted. This book analyses the concept of divorce by focusing on the social, political, economic and religious factors influencing the ancient communities. This work will certainly attract a substantial number of readers who will be confronted with a new and challenging look at divorce.

Professor H.A.J. Kruger
Biblical Studies
School of Religion & Theology
University of KwaZulu-Natal
South Africa

FOREWORD

Unassuming persons are usually special gifts to a society. This could also be said about the author. Being conscious of the negative effects, spiritually and ethically, on a large sketch of humanity in this era, the time has arisen to counteract the negative trends that feed the modern era in most parts of the world. Of course, these trends cannot merely be removed by largely meaningless statements. The author has given much attention to the abnormal situations in which many societies find themselves. Abnormality in the human context is so often taken for granted. This is clearly stated by the above mentioned author.

The author gave attention to 'forced divorce'; to divorce as a phenomenon and its effects on people whatever their race, caste, culture or religion is. The author states that he has found in various 'cultures and religions there are different grounds for divorce', this of course is *ipso facto*. Various case studies have been made as indicated in the preface.

The contents of the book are divided into five chapters, each chapter with its special emphasis, namely, Chapter One: The Social Culture of Ancient Israel; Chapter Two: A Background to the Social Crisis in Ezra and Nehemiah; Chapter Three: A Critique for Ezra and Nehemiah's Remedy for the Marriage Crisis; Chapter Four: Kingdom Ethics – Rhetorical Criticism of New Testament Texts; and Chapter Five: The Jewish Provision for Divorce and the Agunah problem.

In Chapter One, the emphasis falls on the family structure in the Biblical Societies such as the 'Fratriarchate' family, the 'Matriarchate' family and the 'Patriarchate' family. Family solidarity and family customs are also adequately discussed. Much attention is given to the social crisis in Ezra and Nehemiah in Chapter Two. Various aspects receive close attention – a truly incisive disposition. Chapter Three renders a critique of Ezra and Nehemiah's remedy for the marriage crisis. Incisive analyses and evaluations are put forward. The analyst is a most meticulous person. Each and every section is meticulously analysed and presented. The analyses are not only effective – these are super effective, in a sense astounding. In Chapter Four, insight into the New Testament world from a cultural anthropological perspective is explored. Matthew, Mark, Luke central are excellently discussed.

This study is not only a fresh contribution to the theme under discussion but in a sense a most remarkable disposition to the theme.

Professor G.C. Oosthuizen
Westville/Durban
KwaZulu-Natal
South Africa

PREFACE

This book focuses on reconciling the apparently irreconcilable differences of the Biblical texts that allow divorce and those prohibit divorce. Although, the *New Testament* references to divorce were ambiguous enough to prevent a rapid consensus within the Church that divorce was wholly unacceptable, it is notable that the Christian debate for and against divorce drew on both texts from the *Old Testament* as well as the *New Testament.* One of the major objectives of this book will be to focus on the return of Ezra and Nehemiah and understand why they mandated the Israelite men to divorce the foreign women, who they had taken to be their wives. The secondary objectives will be to bring about an understanding of divorce in the Ancient Israelite Society, and to understand what motivations influenced their ethical systems, distinguishing them from the pagan nations.

An emphasis of 'divorce' or 'forced divorce' in the present decade is hardly inappropriate, for the family is one of the great moral, social, and political issues that preoccupy theologians, social critics and other intellectuals of the time. The evidence lies in hundreds of conduct-books, sermons, tracts, treatises and theses devoted to all aspects of the family, i.e. marriage and sexuality, status of women etc. The family is portrayed as the basic unit of society, and order within the family is the guarantor of social and political order. The vast provision of literature aims to ensure that individuals understand their integral roles within a smoothly functioning family and emphasizes the importance of marital and family stability for society and polity. Fundamental to these considerations is religion, and particularly in Christianity, marriage is ordained by God and familiar relationships are prescribed by God. Any behaviour that runs counter to harmony in marriage or the family not only threatens social stability but is also regarded as contrary to the Divine Commandments.

The necessity for a book of this nature arises out of a context of our present society being plunged into a state of moral disintegration as the number of divorces rises beyond expected and controllable levels affecting people of all race, caste, culture and religion. There are many issues that can motivate the undertaking of a research of this nature. Some researchers are prompted by personal experiences, others by statistics. My personal motivation was due to the researching of the following case studies.

In August 1996, the Egyptian Court of Cassation, the highest court in the land, gave the final ruling on the internationally monitored case of academic Nasr Abu Zaid. The court forcefully dissolved the marriage of Nasr Abu Zaid and his wife, Ebtehal Yunes, although they wanted to be married. He was accused of being an apostate. With the use of the Family Code: Egypt's Muslim Personal Law (MPL), which disallows the marriage of a Muslim to a Non-Muslim the court mandated a divorce by force of Abu Zaid and his wife Ebtehal Yunes, on the ground that her husband was an apostate. The court found him guilty and the sentence passed against him was 'divorce by force' and exile.

In the analysis of this case study, I have discovered that in various cultures and religions there are different grounds for divorce. After searching the Biblical texts, I have found a similar situation in the books of Ezra and Nehemiah where divorce was mandated for reasons of cultural and religious purity of the Ancient Israelite Nation.

The second case study pertains to the Jewish Law. A husband must consent to give his wife a bill of divorce (*'get'*). If he refuses, the wife remains locked in a non-existence marriage, unable to remarry. There are hundreds, possibly thousands of women trapped in this situation in Israel and throughout the Jewish world. There are two issues, which present a different halachic point that could be used to free women. The first case involved a woman who, as an underage minor, married under duress, only to discover that her husband was a violent person. Two halakoth solutions were presented for releasing her. One was that a marriage under duress was *null* and *void*. The other was that since she had never married her husband had she known he was violent, then the marriage was a mistaken transaction and the marriage contract could be considered *null* and *void*.

The second case involved a battered wife. The team recommended compelling a divorce through the use of sanctions against the husband or considering the marriage a mistaken transaction. Again analyzing the Agunah dilemma has prompted me to search the Biblical scriptures for an answer to my crucial question. Forced Divorce? Can a divorce be mandated? Some of the general questions to be asked in this book will revolve around aspects such as: Is there such a concept as Forced Divorce? On what grounds can a divorce be mandated? Does the Bible make provision for Divorce? If the answer to the last question is positive, then why did Ezra and Nehemiah mandate a divorce? And, is the Old Testament contradicting the New Testament with its provision for divorce?

The material for this book was originally researched at the University of KwaZulu-Natal (UKZN), South Africa. I would like to acknowledge my appreciation to the National Research Foundation (NRF) and the Black Academic Acceleration Programme for developing researchers (BAA) at the University of KwaZulu-Natal for the grants given to conduct this research.

In completing this book, I certainly owe a great debt of gratitude to many people. Firstly, appreciation for the inspiration and motivation of my parents need to be acknowledged. Professor H.A.J. Kruger (UKZN), for supervising this research and the priceless years of mentorship. It is because of his priceless mentoring and inspiration that I have continued the journey into academia. Prof. J.A. Smit (UKZN), for his supervision in methodology and his priceless mentoring in developing the appropriate academic skills to be contextually relevant. To both these professors, I owe a great debt of gratitude which words in this preface cannot fully express.

Prof. P. Kumar (Oxford) for broadening my insight to a new paradigm for comparative religious studies and for his valuable mentoring. Prof. P. Kruger (University of Stellenbosch), for his examination and constructive critique of the research material and Professor G.C. Oosthuizen for his priceless mentorship and continuous encouragement.

Secondly, appreciation to Dr. S.K. Moran (UKZN) for his guidance and the opportunity of conducting my research under his research niche area of Cultural Studies and Identity in Literature. Prof. D.L. Buchner (Canada), for his insight into the *Old Testament* civilization. Prof. J.N.K. Mugambi (University of Nairobi, Kenya), for his time and constructive criticism in the course of his research visit to South Africa. Dr. I. Fisher, for his assistance and guidance in the examination of Jewish literature and his generosity with the usage of his personal library collection.

I pray that this book will foster new insight into the Biblical understanding to the provision and prohibition of divorce for social transformation in the church and society.

D. Chetty
Bluff/Durban
KwaZulu-Natal (South Africa)

CONTENTS

1

THE SOCIAL CULTURE OF ANCIENT ISRAEL

INTRODUCTION

A predominant emerging question in the field of modern Biblical criticism is what role does literary art play in the shaping of Biblical narratives? 'A crucial one!' I shall argue, in attempting an analysis of divorce/forced divorce in the Biblical texts. With a fine modulation from moment to moment, determining in most cases the minute choice of words and reported details, the pace of narration, the small movements of dialogue and a whole network of ramified interconnections in the text.

The impact of literary criticism on Biblical studies has aquainted most scholars with the distinction between real and implied authors, and real and implied readers, and with the need for a proper and precise terminology in analyzing narratives, *i.e.* plot, characterization, point of view, stock-scenes, types and so on.[1] Before I weigh the theoretical considerations that would explain why this should be so, it would be well to follow the sustained operation created by the literary artifact to know its author, time, place and purpose.[2]

Undoubtedly an important element in the exegesis of the Biblical texts is to understand the social context in which it prevailed. This provides the exegete with a background to the structures and institutions of the Ancient Israelite Society. In analyzing the 'ethical pragmatism' of divorce in the Biblical texts, I plan to analyze the institutions of family *viz.* 'The Family Structures in the Biblical Societies', 'Family Solidarity and Family Customs', 'Institutions of Marriage in the Ancient Israelite Society', 'Institutions of Divorce' and 'The Role of Women in the Israelite Society'.

FAMILY STRUCTURES IN THE BIBLICAL SOCIETIES

According to the discoveries made by different ethnographers, there existed several types of families in the ancient societies. Three types of family structures are noted in the Biblical texts *viz*: *'Fratriarchate'*, *'Matriarchate'*, and *'Patriarchal'*.

The 'Fratriarchate' Family

In the *'fratriarchate'* family, the eldest brother is the head of the family. This authority is handed on, along with property, from brother to brother. This type of structure has been found in the societies of the Hittites, Hurrites in Assyria and Elam.[3] A trace of this type of family structure is evident in the *Old Testament.* In Genesis 34, we see the actions of Jacob's sons to avenge the rape of their sister Dinah. In Genesis 24, Laban played an important role in the arrangement of the marriage of his sister Rebecca. Although, these examples are not conclusive proof, it is admitted as a hypothesis that among the Assyrian and Hurrite, there was an existence of the *'fratriarchate'* system in the early times.[4]

The 'Matriarchate' Family

The second type of family in the Biblical text is the *'Matriarchate'*, which were common in the primitive or undeveloped societies. The characteristic mark of this type of family structure is not that the mother exercises authority (which was very rare), but that a child's lineage is traced through the mother. 'The child belongs to the mother's family and social group, and is not considered as related to its father's connections, even rights of inheritance are fixed by maternal descent.'[5] If this type of family structure had existed in the reconstruction of Israel by Ezra and Nehemiah then we can assume that it would have a major impact when the marriages to the foreign women were dissolved.

Several *Old Testament* customs and stories indicate the presence of this regime among the Israelites. In Genesis 20:12, we see that Abraham is excused for passing off Sarah as his sister, because she was in fact his half-sister, whom he had married. In 2 Samuel 13:13, Amnon and Tamar could have been married, although both were

David's children, they both had different mothers. These texts of Sarah and Tamar prove that a marriage to a half-sister was not yet forbidden. In Judges 14, we see a rare type of marriage, where the wife does not leave her clan, but brings her husband into it. This is a relic of the 'Matriarchate' Society.

The 'Patriarchal' Family

Whatever may be true of the epoch of prehistoric Israel, there is no doubt that from the time of the oldest documents, the Israelite family was *'Patriarchal'*.[6] The Hebrew word to describe this structure is *bêth'ab* literally translated as *'the house of one's father'*.[7] The genealogies are given by the father's line, women are rarely mentioned. According to Leviticus 25:49, the nearest relation in the collateral line is the paternal uncle. As a rule, a man and wife found their place in the grouping of the family, to which four generations generally belong. The idea was to secure the continuance of the father's house.[8]

In this family structure, the husband is the *Ba'al* of his wife, translated as *'Master'*, with absolute authority over his children, over his married sons, if they lived with him and over their wives.[9] The family consisted of those who were united by *common blood* and common-dwelling place.[10] According to Nehemiah 7:4, the *'family'* is a *'house'* – *bêth*, to find a family is to *'build a house'*. In a wider sense the family was the same group as the *'clan'*, the *mishpahah.* They were concentrated in one area, occupying one or more villages according to its size (e.g. the *mishpahah* of the Danites at Soreah and Eshtaol – Judges 18:11. Alternatively, several *mishpahôth* might live together within a city, like the groups from Judah and Benjamin listed in the census of Jerusalem by Nehemiah – Nehemiah 11:4-8).[11] In 1 Samuel 20:29, the clan shared common interests and duties and were united by a blood bond.

FAMILY SOLIDARITY AND FAMILY CUSTOMS

The *'family solidarity'* is seen above all in the group's duty to protect its weak and oppressed members. This obligation lies behind the institution of the *go'el*. The Hebrew word *go'el* comes from the root, which means *'to buy back'*, *'to redeem'*, *'to claim to'*, but fundamentally its meaning is *'to protect'*.[12] This custom can be seen in the story of Ruth, *i.e.* *'the redemption of patrimony'*. Another obligation of the *go'el* was blood vengeance. The honour and dishonour of every member affects the entire group. The blood of a kinsman must be avenged by the death of one who shed it, or failing him, by the blood of one of his family.[13]

These family ties were an inheritance from tribal organizations. The transition to settled life, and the development of town life, brought about social changes, which affected family customs.[14] The family ceased to be self-sufficient, because the standard of material welfare rose and the development of industries led to a specialization of activities. However, the idea of the blood bond was still significant, crafts were handed on from father to son, the reservation of priesthood to families of the tribe of Levi was still a general practice.[15]

INSTITUTIONS OF MARRIAGE IN THE ANCIENT ISRAELITE SOCIETY

Polygamy and Monogamy

In Genesis 2:21-24, the creation of the first two human beings, Adam and Eve, was presented as God's original plan for mankind, *i.e.* a monogamous marriage. Polygamy first appeared in the reprobate line of Cain, when Lamech took two wives (Genesis 4:19). Genesis 1 and 2, apparently showed God's original plan for humanity as one man to one woman for life. However, it was not long before a code of rules was needed because the standards of society had fallen. In this connection the law-code of King Hammurabi of Babylon (about 1700 BC) stipulated that:

(a) 'A man would not take a second wife unless the first was unable to have children.
(b) The husband was allowed a secondary wife (a concubine), or his wife might give him a slave-girl, to have children by her.
(c) The children of the slave-girl, shall not be sent away.'[16]

It is clear that Abraham observed these customs. Abraham at first only had one wife, Sarah, and because she was barren, he took her slave-girl, Haggar (Genesis 16:1-2). (Abraham also married Qeturah, after the death of Sarah - Genesis 23:1-2). Nahor (Genesis 22:20-24) had children by his wife Milkah, and also had a concubine, Remuah. This seems to be against the stipulations of King Hammurabi. However, polygamy was becoming a custom of the time.

According to de Vaux, 'The husband can, however, himself take a concubine, even if his wife has borne him children, but the concubine never has the same rights as his wife, and he may not take a second concubine unless the first is barren.'[17] In the Fifteenth Century BC, in the region of Kirkuk, the same customs were prevalent, but the barren wife was under an obligation to provide a concubine for her husband.[18] In the midst of this polygamy, there was still a relative monogamy because there was only one lawful wife. However, it seems as though the Patriarchs followed a less stringent code of conduct than that which prevailed in Mesopotamia. In Genesis 29:15-30 and 30:1-9, Jacob married the two sisters, Leah and Rachel, each of whom gave him her maid.

However, at the end of the Second Millennium BC, the Assyrian Code of Law, assigned an intermediary place between the wife and the concubine, who is a slave, to the *esirtu (woman of the harem).* A man may have several *esirtu* and they may be raised to the rank of a wife. Later the Talmud fixed the number of wives at four for a subject and eighteen for a king.[19]

It is clear, however, that the most common form of marriage in the Israelite society was monogamy. In the books of Samuel and Kings, which cover the entire period of the monarchy, there is not a single case recorded of bigamy among the commoners, (except that of Samuel's father, at the very beginning of the period). Also, the wisdom books, which provide a picture of the ancient society, never mentions polygamy.[20]

An Israelite Marriage

The married woman came under the authority of her husband. According to the *Decalogue* (Exodus 20:17 – The *Decalogue* contains the words of Yahweh which were the precepts for religion and life in Israel), the wife is listed among the man's possession.[21] In Deuteronomy 21:13, 24:1, to *'marry a wife'* is expressed by the

Hebrew verb *ḥâ`al,* the root meaning of which is to *'become a master'*. However, the question that now arises is whether a wife is really the property of her husband, in other words, had he bought her? Ethnographers have suggested that the Israelites practiced a form of *'Marriage by Purchase', i.e. 'A Purchase-Theory'.*[22] This theory can be substantiated by the custom of the *mohar* (dowry/bride-price).

The Mohar

The *'mohar'* was a sum of money, which was paid to the father of the bride in exchange for the hand of his daughter in marriage.[23] The amount of the *mohar* varied and depended on the father of the girl and the social standing of the family. Payment of the *mohar* could be compound by service, *e.g.* like Jacob did for both his wives (Genesis 29:15-30).

Alternatively, by accomplishing an appointed task, as David did for Michal (1 Samuel 18:25-27). David demonstrated a becoming modesty (1 Samuel 18:18-23), which was intertwined with his inability to pay the *mohar* appropriate for a King's daughter. The *mohar* was one hundred foreskins of the Philistines – The task in exchange for the hand of his daughter was to take vengeance on the King's enemies. This obligation to pay a sum of money, or its equivalent, to the girl's family obviously gives the Israelite marriage the outward appearance of a *'purchase'*.

However, there is a difference between compensation given to the family of the bride and the price paid for a woman. The difference becomes clear, if we compare the *mohar* marriage with another type of union, which really was a purchase, *i.e.* a girl could be sold by her father to another man who intended her to be his own, or his son's concubine. Thus, she was a slave, and could be resold.[24]

By marriage a woman left her parents and went to live with her husband and joined his clan. This was the normal custom. In Genesis 24:58-59, Rebecca left her father and mother, in Genesis 24:5-8, Abraham would not allow Isaac to go to Mesopotamia unless the wife chosen for him agreed to come to Canaan. However, there are few cases in the Bible where there was an exception. In Genesis 31: 26, 43, Jacob, after marrying Leah and Rachel, continued to live with his father-in-law, Laban. In Judges 8:31, Gideon had a concubine who continued to live with her family at Shechem, Samson married a Philistine woman of Timnah, the woman continued to live with her parents, where Samson visited her (Judges 14:8ff, 15:1-2). This type of marriage where the wife does not leave her father's house, the husband takes up residence in her home and relinquishes his connections with his own clan, is called a *beena* marriage.[25] Ancient Assyrian law also provided for a case where a married woman continued to live with her father, this type of marriage was called *erebu.*[26]

Choosing a Bride

The Bible stipulated no age at which a girl could be married. However, for centuries the custom in the East was for boys and girls to be married while they were very young.[27] In the later days, the Jewish Rabbis fixed the minimum age for marriage at twelve years for a girl and thirteen years for a boy. As a result of this practice parents made all the decisions when a marriage was being arranged. In Genesis 24:33-53, Abraham sent his servant to choose a wife for Isaac, the servant arranged the contract with Laban, Rebecca's brother. Only afterwards was Rebecca's consent asked (Genesis 24:57-58). If this analogy is interpreted with certain Mesopotamian texts, then we see that her consent was asked only because her father was dead, and because her brother, not her father had authority over her. Once the proposal of marriage had been put to the girl's parents, they discussed the conditions, especially the amount of the *mohar* (Genesis 29:15ff).

However, parental authority also left room for the feelings of the young couple. In Genesis 34:4/Judges 14:2, we note that the young man could make his preference known. Sometimes, he could make his own decision without consulting his parents, even against their wishes (Genesis 26:34-25).

According to de Vaux '... it was custom to take a wife from among one's own kith and kin, the custom was a relic of tribal life.'[28] In Genesis 24:4, we note that Abraham sent his servant to find Isaac a wife among his own family in Mesopotamia. Laban declared that he would rather give his daughter to Jacob than to a stranger. Tobias also advised his son to choose a wife within his tribe (Tobias 4:12). The counteraction of Samson to the tribal custom, resulted in his father being saddened, because his son did not choose a wife from his own clan.

Marriages also took place between persons of different families and even with foreign women. Esau married two Hittite women,[29] Joseph married an Egyptian,[30] Moses married a Midianite.[31] Naomi's two daughter-in laws were Moabites,[32] David had a Calebite and an Aramaean among his wives.[33] Israelite women were also married to foreigners, Batsheba to a Hittite,[34] and the mother of Hiram, the bronze worker to a Tyrian.[35]

These mixed marriages first started with Kings for political reasons.[36] However, it later became common among the subjects after settlement in Canaan (Judges 3:6). The results of these mixed marriages were firstly that they *'tainted the purity'* of Israel's blood, secondly that they *'endangered its religious faith'* (1 Kings 11:4). And thirdly, they were *'forbidden by law'* (Exodus 34:15-16, Deuteronomy 7:3-4).[37]

An exception was made for women who were captured in wars. The Israelites could marry these women after a ceremony symbolizing the abandonment of their country of origin was performed.[38] However, little respect was paid to these prohibitions. The community, which returned from exile, continued to contract mixed marriages (Malachi 2:11-12). Ezra and Nehemiah both had to take strict measures to counteract these problems. Within the family, marriages with very close relations were forbidden. According to Leviticus 18:6, one does not unite with the *'flesh of one's blood'*. These bans amount to the prohibition of incest. The main collections of these precepts are found in Leviticus 18.

Special restrictions were subjected to members of the priestly line. According to Leviticus 21:7, they could not take a wife who had been a prostitute, or divorced by her husband. For High Priests, the rules were stricter; he could only marry a 'virgin of Israel'.[39]

ENGAGEMENTS AND MARRIAGE CEREMONIES

The Hebrew word *'aras'* literally meaning *'engagement'* or *'betrothal'*, was a promise of marriage made sometime before the celebration of the wedding, according to the custom of Israel. Legal texts show that engagements were a recognized custom with *'Judicial consequences'*.[40] According to Deuteronomy 20:7, a man who was engaged, though not yet married, was excused from going to war. In 1 Samuel 18:21, we see the formula that was probably spoken by the girl's father to make the engagement valid: *'Today you shall be my son-in-law.'*[41]

According to de Vaux, 'in Israel and Mesopotamia, marriage was a purely civil contract'.[42] It was not sanctioned by any religious act. In Malachi 2:14, the bride is called the *berîth – 'the wife of the Covenant'*. The Hebrew analogy of *berîth* is often used to denote a religious pact, but it should be interpreted in the above text as simply a contract of marriage. In Proverbs 2:17, marriage is called the *'Covenant of God'*. This is based on the allegory of Ezekiel 16:8, where the Covenant of Sinai becomes the contract of marriage between Yahweh and Israel.

It was custom among the Jews that a contract of marriage had to be signed.[43] In Tobias 7:13, a written contract of marriage is mentioned. According to the Code of Hammurabi,[44] a marriage concluded without a contract is invalid. The formula pronounced at marriage according to the Elephantine contract was: *'She is my wife and I am her husband, from this day forever.'*[45]

In assessing the early Israelite sociology for marriage, we should note that it was originally better, in close contracts of life for every marriageable woman to be in proper relationship to some man, rather than that improper relationships should arise in which the children would suffer because no one would be responsible for them.[46]

INSTITUTIONS OF DIVORCE

Provision for Divorce

According to the motivation given in Deuteronomy 24:1, a man could divorce his wife if he had *'found some unseemly thing in her'*. There was great debate in the Rabbinical Age concerning the meaning of the above phrase. The school of Rabbi Shammai acknowledged only adultery and misconduct for the grounds of divorce.[47] The more liberal school of Rabbi Hillel acknowledged that if a wife cooked a bad dish or that the husband had found another woman, which he preferred, he could ask for a divorce.[48]

Procedure of Divorce

In the procedure of divorce, the husband made out a declaration contradicting that which had sealed the marriage, *i.e. 'She is no longer my wife and I am no longer her husband'.*[49] In Assyria the formula for a divorce was :*'I repudiate her'* or *'You are no more my wife'.*[50] However, in Israel, Mesopotamia and Elephantine, they also practiced a custom in which the husband had to write his wife a certificate/bill/ writ of divorce, which allowed a woman to remarry.[51]

Restrictions for Divorce

There were a few laws, which were laid to restrict the husband from the right of a divorce. According to Deuteronomy 22:13-19, if a man had falsely accused his wife of not being a virgin when he married her, he could not divorce her. Deuteronomy 22:28-29 stipulates that if a man had violated a girl, he was compelled to marry her.[52] If a divorced wife remarried and later her second husband died or liberated her by a divorce, the first husband was forbidden to take her back.[53] With David and Michal, this law did not apply. Michal was first married to David, then given to another man, and finally taken back by David, however, David had never divorced her (1 Samuel 18:20-27, 25:44, 2 Samuel 3:13-16).

Women had no right to ask for a divorce. At the beginning of the Christian era, when Salome, the sister of Herod sent her husband Kostabar a letter of divorce, her actions were held to be against Jewish law.[54] If the Gospel made reference to a woman divorcing her husband, it was the influence of Gentile customs.[55]

According to the Code of Hammurabi, that prevailed in Mesopotamia, a husband could divorce his wife by pronouncing the appropriate formula, but he had to pay her compensation. In Assyrian law, the husband had the right to divorce his wife without any compensation. However, this led to the Assyrian marriage being complicated, because they often stipulated more onerous conditions for the husband. When the marriages were arranged, the wife's parents might protect her interests by special clauses.[56]

Although the *Old Testament* makes no reference to financial conditions attached to divorce, it is likely that Israel also practiced some kind of remuneration. According to stipulations in the marriage contract of Elephantine, a husband could not reclaim the *mohar* he had paid for his wife, it becomes the *'price of divorce'*.[57]

THE ROLE OF WOMEN IN THE ISRAELITE SOCIETY

In the book of Proverbs we find that two female figures illustrate the role a woman played in the Israelite society. Firstly, we are introduced by the texts to the *'Woman Wisdom'*. She is seen as a divine personification whose moral, intellectual and erotic appeal allures the male into pursuit of her. Secondly, we are introduced to a *'Strange woman'* or *'Foreign woman'*, she is regarded as a negative anti-type of *'Woman wisdom'*. Camp emphasizes the multivalence of the *'Strange woman'* as a symbol of chaos threatening the established social, economic, religious and moral orders.[58]

There were two sides of this ancient *Madonna*, each highly charged erotically, but standing in tension with one another, one accessible but dangerous, the other remote and ethereal, both functioning ideologically within the Israelite society. Any woman that wielded her sexual powers outside the male-governed arrangements of marriage and family are construed as fundamentally the *'Strange Woman'* in Proverbs 1-9. According to Camp, this *'Strange woman'*, was seen as a force that will ultimately split the religious cosmos of Judaism into a dualistic moral system.[59]

As we have seen before in the situation of marriage, the husband is the *ba'al* or *'master'*, the wife addressed him as a slave addressed his master. However, the wife of an Israelite was not on the level of a slave. If a woman in public view was not patently accountable to a man, she was liable to be presumed a prostitute.[60] According to Exodus 21:7, a man could sell his daughter but, a man could never sell his wife (Deuteronomy 24:14).

A husband had the right to divorce his wife, but she was protected by the certificate of divorce (*get)*, which guaranteed her freedom. Within the family, respect for a wife increased on the birth of her first child. This respect was even greater if the child was a boy.[61] The wisdom literature emphasized that respect should also be given to the mother by the children, *i.e.* the same respect given to the father should be given to the mother (Proverbs 19:26, 20:20, 23:22, 30:17).

Milgrom notes that in the description of the woman's suspected unfaithfulness (adultery), the word for her transgress is *ma'al*. This is the only time that the term is used outside the sacred sphere of the *oath violations*,[62] where the object of the *ma'al* is invariably the Deity. He goes on to remind us that the unfaithful wife is a recurring prophetic image for Israel's infidelity to God. Milgrom cites Hosea 2:4-22, Jeremiah 3:8ff, Ezekiel 23:37, on Israel as the sinning wife. *Ma'al* is used in the priestly texts for idolatry extended to straying after other gods.[63]

The ceremony for a woman whose husband suspects her of adultery without proof is to take the woman before a priest. She drinks the words of a curse mixed in water with the dust of the floor of the tabernacle. If she is wrongly suspected, she goes away free. The husband must then stop being jealous. If we interpret the right straightforwardly as a law, the book of Numbers tells the husband that without evidence he cannot take action against his wife. Only the Lord knows and the question of guilt has to be left without the outcome of the ordeal. If she is guilty, then the Lord will punish her by affliction.[64]

The social and legal position of the Israelite wife was inferior to the position a wife occupied in the other countries surrounding Israel.[65] In Egypt it was custom that the wife was the head of the family, in Babylon, the wife could purchase property, take legal action, be a party to contracts, and she even had a share in her husband's inheritance. In the Colony of Elephantine, the Jewish wife acquired certain civil rights. Since she owned property, she also became liable to taxation.[66]

These countries differed from the role an Israelite woman played in her society. The Israelite woman had to do all the hard works at home. Her role was to look after the flock, cook the food, do the spinning, etc.[67] However, these tasks did not lower her status but rendered her sincere consideration, as a vital and important member in the family structure. Many feminist theologians may argue that this picture of the Israelite woman, is a subordination to man, within a system of women oppression. However, one needs to take into consideration that it was custom in the Israelite society to be submissive to the authority of the man, who is the head of the family.[68]

CONCLUSION

Gottwald defined the society depicted in the Bible as a real historical society.[69] The literature (Biblical Texts) is a product of that society, the literature's form and ideas, as well as its descriptions of society and history, offer direct evidence of that society's culture. The encouragement of local religious and cultural identities was part of the imperial strategy.[70] The Biblical writings are one of the results of this initiative.

As discussed in this chapter, Israel had a unique family structure. The several institutions of family such as the nature of the family, marriage, divorce, the role of women etc. differed from pagan societies. These unique institutions and structures gave Israel its own family identity. The community, tribe and clan were seen as an extension to the small immediate family unit.

Various Biblical passages depict that the family was an important component of the Israelite society as an entity. In the creation of a unique family identity of the Israelite nation, solidarity to family and tribal organizations, together with family customs were of vital importance.

The institutions of marriage were also unique. A monogamous marriage with a polygamous nature. The men had one lawful wife, but also several concubines. The marriage was sanctioned by the payment of the *mohar*. Choosing a bride was a very special occasion. The link in the family bloodline was of vital importance. Brides were commonly chosen amongst their own tribe and family. This ensured the continuation of the family blood genealogy and also wealth circulated within the family.

With the institution of marriage, there was also the institution of divorce. This right was granted to the man. He had the right to discontinue his marriage. However, there were certain restrictions. The issuing of a *'get'* (a certificate of divorce), guaranteed the woman her freedom to remarry.

The women in the Israelite society also had a unique identity in comparison to the surrounding countries. The rights of the women varied considerably to that of the Babylonians, Egyptians, Mesopotamians and Elephantines. This difference ensured that the unique family structure of Israel still prevailed. However, these family structures were soon to be challenged. When the Israelites returned from exile in Babylon, several mixed marriages were contracted, *i.e.* marriages to foreign women. The contracting of mixed marriages brought influences of mixed cultures, mixed religions, mixed morality, mixed family structures etc. The product of these marriages were a fragmentation to Israel's unique identity. It tainted the purity of Israel's blood, endangered Israel's religious faith, it was forbidden by law. It also began to fragment the original unique family identity created within the Israelite society.

However, in considering these facts, the questions that now arise relates to my hypothesis of forced divorce, *i.e.* were the actions of Ezra and Nehemiah justified? Was mandating a divorce really necessary in reconstructing a new Israel? Williamson stated that 'the treatment described in Ezra of how he tackled the problem of mixed marriages is among the least attractive parts of Ezra and Nehemiah, if not the whole *Old Testament*'.[71] Similarly Clines was appalled by the personal misery brought into so many families by the compulsory divorce of foreign wives and outraged at Ezra's insistence on racial purity, which is uncongenial to modern liberal thoughts.[72]

NOTES

1. Alter R, *The Art of Biblical Narrative*, George Allen & Unwin, London, 1981, p.3.
2. Davies RP, *In search of Ancient Israel, Journal for the Study of Old Testament,* Supplement Series 148, JSOT Press, Sheffield, 1992, pp.11-12.
3. Roland de Vaux, *Ancient Israel- Its Life and Institutions*, Darton, Longman and Todd, London, 1965, pp.19-21.
4. Ibid. p.19.
5. Ibid. p.19.
6. Ibid. p.20.
7. Ibid. p.20.
8. Wolf HW, *Anthropology of the Old Testament*, Fortress Press, Philadelphia, 1974, p.166.
9. Roland de Vaux, *Ancient Israel- Its Life and Institutions*, Darton, Longman and Todd, London, 1965, p.20.
10. Ibid. p.10. The bond of blood, real or supposed, creates certain solidarity among all members of the tribe – extended family.
11. Ibid. p.21.
12. Ibid. p.21.
13. Ibid. pp.10-11.
14. Ibid. p.22.

15. Ibid. p.22.
16. Alexander P. *(et al.)*, *The Lion Concise Bible Encyclopedia*, Lion Publishing, England, 1980, p.164 – *see marriage.*
17. Roland de Vaux, *Ancient Israel - Its Life and Institutions*, Darton, Longman and Todd, London, 1965, p.24.
18. Ibid. p.24.
19. Ibid. p.25.
20. Ibid. p.25.
21. Legally man counts as being the owner of his wife, and the wife is considered as the husband's possession. Wolf HW, *Anthropology of the Old Testament*, Fortress Press, Philadelphia, 1974, p.168.
22. Roland de Vaux, *Ancient Israel - Its Life and Institutions*, Darton, Longman and Todd, London, 1965, p.26.
23. Ibid. p.26. An African equivalent to the *'mohar'* is the 'lobola-bogadi', the seal that bonds the marriage and subsequent relationships. (Setiloane, GM – *Oh God, My Mother, Please Help*, to be published) A similar custom with the same name ('mahr') is found among the Palestinian Arabs today. A parallel though not identical, custom existed in Ancient Babylon – 'Tirhatu'
24. Ibid. p.28.
25. Ibid. pp.28-29.
26. Ibid. p.29.
27. Ibid. p.29.
28. Ibid. p.30.
29. *See* Genesis 26:34.
30. *See* Genesis 41:45.
31. *See* Exodus 2:21.
32. *See* Ruth 1:4.
33. *See* 2 Samuel 3:3.
34. *See* 2 Samuel 11:3.
35. *See* 1 Kings 7:13-14.
36. Roland de Vaux, *Ancient Israel - Its Life and Institutions*, Darton, Longman and Todd, London, 1965, p.31.
37. Ibid. p.31.
38. Ibid. p.31.
39. Ibid. p.32.
40. Ibid. p.32.
41. The custom of engagement also existed in Mesopotamia, and was concluded by the payment of the *tirhatu,* the equivalent to the *mohar*.
42. Ibid. p.33.
43. Ibid. p.33.
44. For the Code of Hammurabi *see*: Pritchard JB, *The Ancient Near East: An Anthology of Texts and Pictures*, Princeton University Press, England, 1958, pp.138-166.
45. Roland de Vaux, *Ancient Israel - Its Life and Institutions*, Darton, Longman and Todd, London, 1965, p.33.
46. Wolf HW, *Anthropology of the Old Testament*, Fortress Press, Philadelphia, 1974, p.169.
47. Roland de Vaux, *Ancient Israel - Its Life and Institutions*, Darton, Longman and Todd, London, 1965, p.34.

48. Landman I, *The Universal Jewish Encyclopedia*, (Volume 3), KTAV Publishing, New York, 1941, pp. 577-579.
49. Roland de Vaux, *Ancient Israel- Its Life and Institutions*, Darton, Longman and Todd, London, 1965, p.35.
50. Ibid. p.35.
51. Ibid. p.35. A writ of divorce dating from the beginning of the Second Century of our era was found in the caves of Murrabba'at.
52. Singer I, *The Jewish Encyclopedia*, (Volume 4) KTAV Publishing House, New York, (n.d.), pp. 624-625.
53. Roland de Vaux, *Ancient Israel - Its Life and Institutions*, Darton, Longman and Todd, London, 1965, p.35.
54. Ibid. pp.35-36.
55. Ibid. pp.35-36.
56. Ibid. p.36.
57. Ibid. p.36.
58. Camp C, *Wisdom and the Feminine in the book of Proverbs*, (Bible and Literature) Volume 11, Almond Press, Sheffield, 1985, p.199, cf. pp.112 – 120.
59. Ibid. p.120.
60. Bird P, *The Harlot as Heroine: Narrative Art and Social Presupposition in Three Old Testament Texts*, Semeia 46, 1989, pp.120 –121. Bird describes the prostitute's marginal status as the consequence of men's conflicting claims both to exclusive control of their wives' sexuality and sexual access to other women. Her social status was that of an outcast, though not an outlaw. She seemed like a tolerated, but dishonored, member of society. The harlot was the other woman that was stigmatized, desired by men but ostracized.
61. Roland de Vaux, *Ancient Israel- Its Life and Institutions*, Darton, Longman and Todd, London, 1965, p.39.
62. Milgrom J, *Numbers, The JPS Torah Commentary*, Jewish Publication Society, Philadelphia, 1990, p.37.
63. Ibid. p.37.
64. Douglas M, *In The Wilderness: The Doctrine of Defilement in the Book of Numbers, Journal for the Study of Old Testament,* Supplement Series 158, Sheffield Academic Press, England, 1993, pp. 160-171.
65. Roland de Vaux, *Ancient Israel - Its Life and Institutions*, Darton, Longman and Todd, London, 1965, p.39.
66. Ibid. p.39.
67. Ibid. p.39.
68. Ibid. p.39.
69. Gottwald NK, *The Tribes of Yahweh: A Sociology of the Religion of the Liberated Israel*, Orbis Books, Maryknoll, New York, 1979.
70. Ezkenazi TC, Richard HK, *Second Temple Studies: 2 Temple and Community in the Persian Period*, Sheffield Academic Press, England, 1994, pp. 23-27.
71. Williamson HGM, *Ezra -Nehemiah*, Word, Waco, Texas, 1985, p.159.
72. Clines DJA, *Ezra, Nehemiah and Ester*, Eerdmans, Grand Rapids, Michigan, 1984, p.116.

2

A BACKGROUND TO THE SOCIAL CRISIS IN EZRA & NEHEMIAH

INTRODUCTION

Although the Israelite nation had a unique family structure giving them their own family identity, a situation in the post-exilic community called for the implementation of divorce by force. In understanding the reasons for these actions that seem to undermine the legitimacy of the family structure in Israel, let me propose before an actual criticism of the text, an analysis of the historical and literary background to the texts and a sociological background with special reference to the mixed marriage crisis in Ezra and Nehemiah.

A HISTORICAL AND LITERARY BACKGROUND TO THE TEXTS

A coherent reading of any artwork, whatever the medium requires some detailed awareness of the grid of conventions upon which, and against which, the individual work operates. Through our awareness of convention we can recognize significant patterns of repetition, symmetry, contrast, clues in a narrative work and see what is innovative and what is deliberately traditional at each nexus of the artistic creations.[1]

According to Childs, the books of Ezra and Nehemiah formed a single book in the Hebrew canon. The separation into two books was relatively a late development and did not appear in the Hebrew Bible until the late fifteenth century.[2] In terms of literary problems, the relation between the editorial work of the final author and the sources, which he used are not at all clear. The historical problems associated with the writings of Ezra and Nehemiah have caused many scholars to regard the present canonical shape of these books as *'confused and distorted'*.[3] Due to these historical and literary problems that cause a fragmentation, the texts cannot be seen as a whole consistent narrative. Hence, over the years scholars have developed a *'Source Theory'* to explain these differences and inconsistencies.

AN ANALYSIS OF THE SOURCE THEORY

Sectional Deconstruction of Ezra and Nehemiah

Several sections can be clearly defined in the Books of Ezra and Nehemiah. Ezra 1-6 is a description of the circumstances surrounding the returns from exile in Babylon. It focuses on their efforts to re-build the temple in Jerusalem. In Ezra 7-10, there seems to be a fragmentation of time. The reader is introduced to Artaxerxes, who takes the role of a new King in the narrative. He succeeds Cyrus and Darius mentioned in the earlier chapters. Ezra is here authorized by Artaxerxes to go to Jerusalem with treasures for the temple. He received the commission to undertake teachings of the law, reformation and restoration. He learns of the marriage of a number of Jews to foreign women. His response was to establish a commission.

The book of Nehemiah begins with the scene shifting back to the community in exile. However, the date is some thirteen years later in the reign of Artaxerxes. Nehemiah secures permission to return to Jerusalem to help re-build the city. Each section so far followed a pattern of a return from exile, reformation and restoration. The final part of the book, however, appears more complicated. Nehemiah 7 and 11 focus on the re-population of Jerusalem in his time. Nehemiah 12:27-43 focus on the dedication of the newly built city wall. Interspersed in Nehemiah 8-10 and 11:3-12:26 are a presentation of the law by Ezra, followed by a confession and a pledge to keep the law in future, and various lists of residents, priests, Levites and others in Jerusalem. Nehemiah, 13 relates to various incidents during his second term as Governor including the issue of mixed marriages.

In analyzing these literary units, we need to take into account that Ezra and Nehemiah, each tells part of their experience in their own words. The remaining units are in Hebrew and Aramaic.[4]

Literary and Historical Problems in Ezra

The narrative material in Ezra 7-10 and Nehemiah 8, illustrates Ezra as.playing a major character role. However, in these narratives there are switches between the third person and the first person (Ezra 7:1-26 and Ezra 7:27 – 9:15). In considering these literary problems, the question that arises is: did an editor have in front of him Ezra's own account (an Ezra source) from which he copied some parts and rewrote others? [5]

The order of events in the Ezra narrative also seems odd. Considering the texts literally as they stand, Ezra arrived in Jerusalem in the seventh year of Artaxerxes, with a commission to teach and implement the law of God. Within a year he confronted the problem of mixed marriages. However, a full twelve-thirteen years lapsed before he could present the law in fulfilment of his original commission. According to Williamson, this gap in Ezra's career has never been satisfactorily explained.[6]

Critical Responses to these Problems

In response to the above literary and historical problems, modern critical scholarship, have proposed a variety of solutions, which can be briefly summarized as follows. In subjecting Ezra to criticism of its Hebrew style, Torrey concluded that it could not be distinguished from the editorial hand of the author, who was responsible for the works of the Chronicles, Ezra and Nehemiah.[7]

The German scholar Noth, in examining the literary and historical considerations came to believe that the edict of Artaxerxes in Ezra 7:12-26 and the list in 8:1-14 of those who accompanied Ezra on his journey to Jerusalem were both sources which were available to the Chronicler.[8] Noth, Kellerman and der Smitten assigned the Chronicler a very large role and considered him the actual author rather than an editor of sources.[9] Noth's rationale for the disorder of subsequent events was due to theological reasons and the account of the first person reveals an inconsistent imitation of Nehemiah.[10]

The Norwegian scholar Kapelrud undertook a study of the Hebrew style of the Ezra narrative. His deductions were in agreement to Torrey, that it should be attributed to the same hand as that of the Chronicler.

However, he allowed the possibility of some earlier tradition underlying the account.[11]

Mowinckel with a more conservative view than Noth argues that this editor is the Chronicler. He made this conclusion after finding some editorial comments in the Ezra material. Therefore, the Chronicler must have been working on an already existing text, *i.e.* an Ezra source. He substantiates this source of Ezra as being the work of an admirer, who years later wrote up an idealized version of the events for purposes of edification.[12]

Mowinckel argued that the shift between the first and third person narratives did not arise because of earlier sources, but was a stylistic feature of a *'Denkschrift'*. The use of the first person was a device for self-glorification.[13] Kellerman, however, criticized Mowinckel's theory of self-aggrandizement substituting it with the psalmic genre of *'a prayer of an accused person'*, which had first been described by Hans Schmidt.[14]

Despite the argument of these scholars' views, many scholars have held to a more traditional approach. Rudolph accepted that the material about Ezra was originally written by Ezra in the first person throughout in order to give an account of his work to the Persian King.[15] On the basis of these observations and with the Nehemiah material as a parallel, it is not unreasonable to suggest that as a matter of regular protocol, Ezra was obliged to report on his progress after one year. There is no doubt that a copy of such a report should have been available later in Jerusalem and that an editor could have worked it into a larger composition.[16]

An Evaluation of these Critical Responses

In researching the authorship of Ezra and Nehemiah, I have expressed the views of many scholars above. However, with the increasing awareness of Biblical research in our modern day, certain opinions need to be taken into consideration. Firstly, the argument based upon the Hebrew style cannot be regarded as decisive. Recent discoveries since the analysis of Torrey have increased our awareness of the extent to which the Hebrew language developed during the *Old Testament* period. The Babylonian exile in particular was a 'watershed' since after the influence of Aramaic and Iranian as well as other factors, left a clear mark on the Hebrew language.[17] A great deal of what Torrey attributed to the hand of the Chronicler seems to be a general pattern, (*i.e.* literature tradition) of the time.

In considering the edict of the Artaxerxes and the subsequent narratives, there are number of points of detail, such as places and personal names (Ezra 8:15-17). An inventory (Ezra 8:26-27), curious local colour (Ezra 10:9-13), and an unexpected hitch in the preparations for the journey are also mentioned in detail. These facts are clearly not based on an edict, but which also have no other apparent origin but originated from historical memory.

If so, then the editor must have been working with an inherited source rather than working from scratch. In considering the literary problem of the shift from first person to third person, it appears that Williamson has the most suitable explanation. The Chronicler working on an original first person account of Ezra changed some passages into the third person. He no doubt thought it appropriate to introduce Ezra into the narratives in this manner (Ezra 7:1-10). He then used the words of Ezra's benediction (Ezra 7:27-28) as a skillful way to skip over into the first person. He continued with this throughout Chapters 8 and 9, with the exception of 8:35-36, where he may have been 'papering over' the gap caused by his transfer of material to Nehemiah 8. At the end of Chapter 9, he used the device of prayer to revert to the third person. Finally, Nehemiah 8, had obviously to be in the third person to avoid confusion.

The Nehemiah Memoir

Mowinckel pointed out that the 'Nehemiah Memoir' as it had been commonly known, is an inappropriate technical classification.[18] He suggested that the work would be more appropriately compared with a number of Ancient Near Eastern royal inscriptions in which various kings commemorate their achievements.

Another suggestion for the 'Nehemiah Memoir' is that Nehemiah needed to write in order to justify himself to the Persian King.[19] In the most recent study of Nehemiah, Kellerman starts from a position similar to what was mentioned above, but then deduces that the type of Psalm known as the *'prayer of the accused'*, explains the distinctive characteristics of the Nehemiah material.[20]

The following passages in the book of Nehemiah appear to be a first hand account by Nehemiah himself, Nehemiah 1-2; 4-6; 7:1-5; 12:31-43, and 13:4-31. Williamson identified these passages as characterized by lively narrative and forceful style and in particular by some 'idiosyncratic turns of phrase,'(*i.e.* prayers that God will *remember* Nehemiah for good or his enemies for ill).[21] However, these passages cannot be seen as a single and coherent narrative, there are some gaps in the account. In Nehemiah 3, there is a long list of those who participated in the building of the wall. The question that arises is whether Nehemiah compiled this list. We note that it displays a number of differences from his account. An example can be seen in Chapter 3:1,3,6, whereas, in Chapter 6:1 this stage had not yet been reached.

Far more controversial is the list of names in Chapter 7:6-73. In the previous verses Nehemiah stated that in order to encourage more Judeans to live in Jerusalem, he found 'the genealogy of those who came up at the first'. Following these verses is a list, which is the same as the list in Ezra 2. Williamson noted that the majority of the scholars doubt whether Nehemiah would have included it in his account.[22]

Nehemiah 8-10, are obviously not part of Nehemiah's own account. The question of repopulating Jerusalem in 7:5ff is only picked up at the start of Chapter 11. Due to Chapter 11 not being written in the first person, most commentators believe that this is a portion of the memoir, which was rewritten by a later editor.[23] Apart from the different style of writing, Chapter 11:1-2 differs with Chapter 7. In Chapter 7, Nehemiah is all set to deal with the problem on the basis of family lists. However, in 11:2 it is decided on the arbitrary basis of casting lots. It is not difficult to see why there is a general agreement that the book of Nehemiah includes an authentic first-person account by Nehemiah of his activities relating to Jerusalem.[24] However, with this deduction we note that there are also curious features of some other external source.

Dating Ezra/Nehemiah

The issue concerning the dating of Ezra and Nehemiah has marked great difficulty in the minds of many prominent scholars. This is a vast field and extends outside the boundaries of the present book. However, I have summarized below a few theories of dating these books that would allow for critical discussion.

Williamson argued that there is 'no secure method for dating a work such as Ezra and Nehemiah'.[25] According to the theory of Rudolph, who accepted that the whole of Ezra and Nehemiah were part of the work of the Chronicler, saw no reason to set a date later than 400 BC.[26] However, many scholars tend to disagree with the above dating, considering that Ezra only came to Jerusalem in 398 BC.

Another deduction concerns the reference to the High Priest Jaddua (Nehemiah 12:11 and 12:22) frequently linked with the mention in Josephus (*Jewish Antiquities*),[27] of a high priest of that name who held office at the time when the Persian rule gave place to Hellenistic rule. Therefore, the books as a whole cannot be dated before the Hellenistic Period (late fourth century BC onwards). The mention of mixed marriages brings us to a point, which has been frequently advanced by many scholars as a strong argument for dating Ezra after Nehemiah. In Nehemiah 13:23-27, Nehemiah deals with some isolated instances of this abuse. His approach was said to be unsuccessful and so Ezra was later obliged to deal with the problem more systematically. According to Williamson, it is not just that Nehemiah dealt with a few cases. We should rather consider that they were extremely localized. Reference was made only to the women of Ashdod, Ammon, and Moab.[28] However, considering the crisis of mixed marriage in the post-exilic Judean society, one tends to agree with Williamson that it makes more sense to suppose that Ezra had already dealt with the problem as a whole, and that Nehemiah was merely dealing with the isolated cases of its resurgence.

Chronological Order of Ezra and Nehemiah

Childs notes that the present structures of Ezra and Nehemiah show a clear mark of intentionality, which an author or editor established.[29] The book of Ezra starts with a date formula of 538 BC and continues with a series of dates to the completion of the temple in 516 BC. Ezra' s arrival is seen in Chapter 7 as the seventh year, first day of the fifth month in the reign of Artaxerxes. The book of Nehemiah also follows a clear chronological sequence from the twentieth year of Artaxerxes to the thirty-second year of his reign.

The major disruption in the chronological sequence occurs in Ezra 4:6-23 with reference to the reign of Darius. The introduction of Darius can be substantiated by trying to illustrate the nature of the continual resistance against the Jews. In sum the present arrangements of the chapters are not simply accidental, but reflect a purposeful chronological pattern.

A STUDY OF THE SOCIOLOGY OF THE MIXED MARRIAGE CRISIS IN THE POST-EXILIC JUDEAN COMMUNITY

In the above sections, important features were highlighted in the historical and literary background to the texts, which either directly or indirectly impinge on the exegesis of Ezra and Nehemiah. However, an analysis of the historical and literary background to the texts is not entirely sufficient to ensure a proper exegesis. There are other important dynamics envisaged in the texts that need to be considered.

Therefore, in considering the issue of forced divorce to the foreign women, embodied in mixed marriages, it is of vital importance to consider the sociological background to the texts, (*i.e.* the ideology towards foreign women and mixed marriages in that particular society).

A CRITICAL ANALYSIS OF THE 'STRANGE WOMAN' IN THE WISDOM LITERATURE AND THE POST-EXILIC JUDEAN COMMUNITY

If we define ideology as a cultural formation or a cultural production that expresses a point of view of a social class, it is evident that there existed an ideology towards the 'Strange Woman' in Proverbs and the post-exilic Judean community. Boström suggested that the 'Strange Woman' was not an ordinary prostitute, but a foreign devotee to the goddess Ishtar who engaged in cultic prostitution as a fertility rite.[30] Van der Toorn offered an alternate scenario that the ' Strange Woman' was far from being a professional prostitute. She was instead engaged in an extraordinary act of prostitution for the sake of paying a vow. For Ancient Israelite women living in the margin of the official cult, the vow was a popular form of devotion. Women were typically dependent upon the men to supply the means of payment. However, if a husband or father refused, one of the few means of access to resources (*i.e.* funds to pay the vow) was incidental prostitution.[31] Whatever its merits, Van der Toorn's reading together with Boström's theory, cannot be applied to the larger complex of the 'Strange Woman' passages.

Taking into consideration that Proverbs can be dated in the post-exilic period,[32] scholars have concluded that the woman in Proverbs 1-9, portrayed as a prostitute, can be a reference to the foreign women of the land.[33] Washington argued that the warning in Proverbs 1-9 against unfamiliar women was already a theme for the post-exilic sages.[34]

In a more recent study Camp developed the hypothesis that the 'Strange Woman' figure portrays a 'force defined as a female that will ultimately split the religious cosmos of Judaism and Christianity into a dualistic moral system'.[35]

With these broader interpretative issues in view, I propose to describe the particular social and economic factors that originally motivated the polemic against the foreign women in the post-exilic community. In agreement with the hypothesis of Washington, during the post-exilic period, the 'Strange Woman' was a representation of the women who did not belong to the *'golah'* (community). Relationships between the Judean men and the foreign women posed economic problems. Due to land tenure and cultic membership being linked to genealogical lineage, the prospect of exogamous marriages brought the danger of outside encroachment upon the land holdings of the Judean congregation.[36] As a result Judean men were forbidden to marry foreign women not only for moral and religious reasons, but also because they were a threat to the social and economic integrity of the Judean community.

However, this conventional hypothesis needs relevant substantiation. In order to prove this hypothesis, an analysis of the semantic linguistics in the Biblical texts for the application of the 'Strange Woman' needs to be investigated.

EXAMINING THE SEMANTIC LINGUISTICS IN THE USAGE OF THE TERM 'STRANGE WOMAN'

Under the grouping of *zarah*, the Wisdom Literature (*i.e.* Proverbs

1-9), gathers an assortment of warnings against unfamiliar women. Due to the composite nature of her portrayal, the prescribed figure has no consistent identity. The woman according to Yee is depicted as *'alien, harlot, evil, adulterous and foolish'*.[37] However, the essential attribute unifying the accounts of the forbidden woman is her designation as *zarah/nakryah* ('strange').

To ascertain the motivation of the sage for denouncing her, the semantic value of these terms need to be examined. According to Biblical Hebrew the adjective *zar* denotes *'otherness'* referring to what is outside the field of recognition or legitimacy.[38] In Exodus 30:9, we find a reference to *'illicit (zarah) incense'* and in Leviticus 10:1 *'unlawful (zarah) fire'*. In these texts, the reference to *zar* is in the cultic context. As a sociological designation *zar* refers explicitly to those outside the pertinent kinship group, whether family, tribe or nation. Thus, the law of the Levirate marriage stipulates that 'the wife of the deceased shall not be married outside (*i.e.* the family, tribe or clan) to a stranger' (Deuteronomy 25:5).

According to the priestly rules of Numbers 3:10, men of non-Aaronic descent, or those outside the tribe of Levi (Numbers 1:51, 18:4) are referred to as *zar*. In the prophetic literature the term *zar* denotes non-Israelites, often used to denote the enemies of Israel (*e.g.* Ezekiel 31:12 *'foreigners' from the most terrible nations*).

A similar range of meanings to those of *zar* is found in the adjective *nakry*. In Psalms 69:9 *nakry* is used to denote *'strangeness'* to the household. However, as a social designation, *nakry* denotes foreignness by reason of nationality or ethnicity.[39] The following texts express this concept, Exodus 21:8, Deuteronomy 17:15, Deuteronomy 29:21, Judges 19:12 and 1King 8:41. In the exilic and post-exilic contexts the words *zar/nakry* are prominent, especially in the prophetic literature where it designates the foreign opponents of Judah, *e.g.* Jeremiah 5:19.

In the Wisdom Literature (*i.e.* Proverbs 1-9), the usage of *zarah* with *nakryah* suggests that the terminology is a reference to a foreign adversary of the Judean community. In comparison with Proverbs 1-9, are Ezra 10:2, 10-11, 14, 17-18, 44 and Nehemiah 13:26-27, where *nakryah* (*i.e.* 'strange') refers to women outside of the community whom men within the Israelite community had married.

I will now attempt to prove that the original context of Proverbs disparagement of the 'Strange Woman' was linked to Ezra and

Nehemiah's drive to free the post-exilic community from everything foreign. Camp suggested that while deviant sexuality was pre-eminent in the earlier tradition of warnings against the 'Strange Woman', the secondary interpretation of the 'strange' (*i.e. zarah/nakryah)* as ethnically foreign came to the fore in support of the post-exilic marriage reforms of Ezra and Nehemiah.[40]

THE SOCIAL-HISTORICAL CONTEXT OF THE POST-EXILIC POLEMIC AGAINST THE FOREIGN WOMEN (LAND TENURE ISSUE)

Prominent scholars have conventionally portrayed that the motive for the prohibition of mixed marriages in post-exilic Judah was to preserve authentic Yahwist observance against syncreticist influences of the people of the land.[41] However, the post-exilic community was not only a religious association.

According to the thesis of Weinberg, the post-exilic Judean community was organized as a *Bürger-Tempel-Gemeinde* (*i.e. Civic-Temple Community*), a religio-political unit fictively constituted as an agnatic lineage of property-holding men and their families.[42] According to Ezra 1:5, 2:59, and Nehemiah 7:70-71, 11:13, membership in the temple community was determined by descent within a paternal estate, *i.e.* property was distributed according to the divisions of this lineage. This implied that in the *Bürger-Tempel-Gemeinde*, participation in the temple cult, land tenure and citizenship were linked under the leadership of the heads of the paternal estates.[43]

The deportees to Babylon comprised only a small proportion of the Judean population. According to 2 Kings 25:12, and Jeremiah 39:10, 40:4-12, after the deportation, the remaining Judean majority appears to have made claims to the land holdings left behind by the exiles. As members of the community began to return and re-establish themselves, conflict over the land was inevitable. Thus, the land tenure was a critical issue for the early post-exilic Judean community.

In response to the local opposition, the returning exiles conceived themselves (typologically) as the generation of a new conquest (Ezra 9:1-2, 10-15). The true Israel, now identified with the community (Ezra 1:11, 2:1, 9:4, Nehemiah 7:6), had entered the land from the outside, and those presently occupying the land were excluded from the covenant community.[44]

The returning community effectively classified the local Judean community (the people of the land), together with their neighbouring non-Judean people (Ammonites, Moabites, Edomites, Samaria etc.), as alien (foreigners) to Israel. Ezekiel 11:15-17 portrays both the non-deported Judeans and the exiles acknowledging that legal right to the land accrues to those with access to the cult (Leviticus 25:23).[45] With an endorsement from the Persian Empire, those who took membership in the re-established *Bürger-Tempel-Gemeinde* secured their legal right to land.[46] Membership into the cult and rights of land were established genealogically. Genealogical reckoning thus, provided an *'ideology of descent'*, which allowed the leaders of the post-exilic community to identify the true Israel, grant membership into the temple, and who would possess land.

Exogamous marriages brought more difficulties in community membership and over land allotments among divisions of the lineage. Marriage alliances had implications on property holdings. This implied that the economic stability of the *Bürger-Tempel-Gemeinde* was vulnerable to disruption by marriages outside the community. Hoglund recognized marriages as a means of transferring property and social status from one group to another and related the marriage reforms of Ezra and Nehemiah to concern over property rights.[47] This can be rendered as a support to Merton's *'exchange theory'*, where we need to consider what *upward* advantages did the foreign women gain by marrying outside the social boundaries of an ethnic group.[48] Undoubtedly, the claim to land was one of the advantages.

Thus, we can understand the emphasis in Proverbs 1-9 and Ezra and Nehemiah on avoiding women outside the community, as it posed a threat to the real property holdings of the Judean collective. As within the patrilineal land tenure system women were capable of inheriting and disposing property (*cf.* Numbers 27:1-11 in the case of the daughters of Zelophehad that inherited land).

The provision for women inheriting land aimed to secure the inheritance within the bounds of its rightful patrilineal tribe. Thus, female heirs were required to marry within the lineage of their late father. These laws, presumably post-exilic in their present form, make clear that it was possible for women to inherit land. This introduced conflicts over the land tenure issue within the Israelite tribe. According to Hoglund, in order for the Persians to facilitate ease of identification for administration and taxation, they enforced a guarded ethnic identity among the returning community, to whom they entrusted regions of the imperial domain.[49] According to this thesis, the returning community risked losing their land entirely if they did not maintain themselves as a distinct community. In sum we can understand why the mixed marriages were perceived as a threat to the survival of the *Bürger-Tempel-Gemeinde.*

THE 'STRANGE WOMAN' AS A THREAT TO THE JUDEAN TEMPLE ECONOMY

In my opinion, the thesis of Washington made an important contribution to the research of *'forced divorce'* with the understanding that the polemic against the '*Foreign/Strange woman*' in Proverbs 1-9, coincided with the ideological strategy of Ezra and Nehemiah.[50] The returning community was classified as a kinship group, anyone outside this community was classified (in the language of ethnicity) as a foreigner, *i.e.* A Judean of illicit background is as alien to the community of Ezra/Nehemiah as an Egyptian or Moabite.

The analogy of the 'Strange Woman' in the Wisdom literature associated with Ezra/Nehemiah, is not only a warning against the foreign women, but with close literary analysis it denotes the consequences of failing to heed to the prohibition. Camp associated the house of the 'Strange Woman' with reference to its sinking (Proverbs 2:18) with the possession of land.[51] Camp builds upon the analogy (Proverbs 2:21), that the *upright*, being those who avoid the 'Strange Woman' will inherit the land, whereas those who seek the 'Strange Woman' shall *be cut off from the land.* The reference to inhabiting the land with the warning against foreign women in Proverbs (Wisdom Literature) reflects the anxiety over land tenure, which was one of the motivating factors in the campaign against mixed marriages in Ezra and Nehemiah.

Proverbs 5:8-10 makes a reference that involvement with the 'Strange Woman' leads to the alienation of Judean wealth. According to Washington, this text related to the fear that Judean property will fall under the control of foreign families, via relationships and eventual marriages to women outside the community.[52] In an analysis of Ezra's established commission to deal with the problem of the mixed marriages (Ezra 10:16), the commission identified and prosecuted those who had married outside the community. The penalties for failure to submit to these proceedings included expulsion from the temple assembly and the confiscation of property.

A comparative analysis in the usage of the term *'property'* in 1 Chronicles 27:31 illustrates the context of the term in Ezra 10:8, to relate to real property, *i.e.* land. In considering that membership into the community entailed the right to own land; the expulsion from the community would mean that they had to forfeit their land to the temple collective. This is why the sages warned in Proverbs 5:14, that if you seek after the 'Strange/Foreign Woman', you will end your life in weakness and poverty and say that *'you were once at the point of utter ruin in the assembly congregation'*.

Thus in sum Hoglund stated that the systems of allocating territories to dependent populations will work as long as the imperial system is capable of maintaining some clarity as to who is allowed access to a particular region and who is not. Intermarriage among various groups would tend to smudge the demarcation between the groups.[53]

CONCLUSION

According to Batten's explanation for the mixed-marriage situation in Ezra and Nehemiah, he motivated that it was due to a scarcity of Jewish women who were returning exiles within the acceptable boundaries of the community.[54] This conception stood in agreement with Rudolph's explication that the ratio was to a disadvantage of young men seeking marriage. They could not find a *'full-blood Jewish woman'* in Palestine.[55]

Ezra defined mixed marriages as a concept of being both ethnically and religiously outside the boundaries of the local community. Merton commented on the attitude of Ezra as it appeared in the Biblical text as being a public outcry against outbursts of moral indignation.[56] On a secondary level, it is important to note that romantic/democratic violations of group identity in mixed marriages result from deviance or alienation from the strictures of a specific ethnic or cultural group.

Undoubtedly, the actions leading to exogamous marriages posed a more complex problem. The land tenure issue, identity crisis, fragmentation of family structures, threats to Judean temple economy and other relevant issues can be substantiated as the reasons for the forced divorce compelled by Ezra and Nehemiah. It is clear that normative social sanctions against mixed marriages sometimes conflict with equally strong values of romantic idealism and can occasionally overcome the group boundaries for some, if not all the persons involved, *i.e.* the couple and the immediate family.

Against a provision of the literary and historical background to the text and a sociological background to the books of Ezra and Nehemiah (with special focus on the ideological conception to foreign women and mixed marriages), I will now focus on an analysis of the texts of Ezra and Nehemiah.

NOTES

1. Alter R, *The Art of Biblical Narrative*, George Allen & Unwin, London, 1981, p.47.
2. Childs BS, *Introduction to the Old Testament as Scripture*, SCM Press, London, 1979, p.626.
3. Ibid. p.627.
4. Williamson HGM, *Ezra and Nehemiah*, (Old Testament Guides), Sheffield Academic Press, England 1987, p.15.
5. Ibid. p.15.
6. Ibid. p.15.
7. Torrey CC, *The Composition and Historical Value of Ezra-Nehemiah*, Beihefte Zur Zaw, Giessen, Ricker, 1896.
8. Over the years scholars have come to call the general editor of Chronicles, Ezra and Nehemiah as a *Chronicler*.
9. Childs BS, *Introduction to the Old Testament as Scripture*, SCM Press, London, 1979, p.629.
10. Noth M, *The Chronicler's History*, Journal for the Study of Old Testament, Supplement Series 50, JSOT Press, Sheffield, 1987.
11. Kapelrud AS, *The Question of Authorship in the Ezra Narrative: A Lexical Investigation*, Oslo, Dybwad, 1944.
12. Williamson HGM, *Ezra and Nehemiah*, (Old Testament Guides), Sheffield Academic Press, England 1987, p.22.
13. Childs BS, *Introduction to the Old Testament as Scripture*, SCM Press, London, 1979, p.627.
14. Ibid. p.628.
15. Williamson HGM, *Ezra and Nehemiah*, (Old Testament Guides), Sheffield Academic Press, England 1987, p.22.
16. Ibid. p.25.
17. Ibid. p.23.
18. Pritchard JB, *Ancient Near Eastern Texts to the Old Testament*, (3rd edition),

Princeton University Press, Princeton, 1969 (Translation to the Ancient Near Eastern Royal Inscriptions).

19. Williamson HGM, *Ezra and Nehemiah*, (Old Testament Guides), Sheffield Academic Press, England 1987, p.18.
20. Emerton JA, *Nehemiah*, Journal for Theological Studies, Series 23, 1972, pp.171-185.
21. Williamson HGM, *Ezra and Nehemiah*, (Old Testament Guides), Sheffield Academic Press, England 1987, p.15. *Koch* argued that the remembrance formula offers the key to understanding the original function of the book, both as a memorial of political self-justification and a prayer for divine vindication. *See* Childs, *The Old Testament as Scripture*, p. 628.
22. Williamson HGM, *Ezra and Nehemiah*, (Old Testament Guides), Sheffield Academic Press, England 1987, p.16.
23. Ibid. p.16.
24. Ibid. p.17.
25. Ibid. p.45.
26. Ibid. p.45.
27. Whiston W (Translator), *The Works of Josephus*, Complete and Unabridged, Hendrickson Publishers, Massachusetts, 1987.
28. Williamson HGM, *Ezra and Nehemiah*, (Old Testament Guides), Sheffield Academic Press, England 1987, p. 65.
29. Childs BS, *Introduction to the Old Testament as Scripture*, SCM Press, London, 1979, p. 631.
30. Ibid. pp. 223-224.
31. Van der Toorn K, *Female Prostitution in Payment of Vows in Ancient Israel*, Journal of Biblical Literature, Volume 108, 1989, p.205.
32. Washington HC, *Wealth and Poverty in the Instruction of Amenemope and the Hebrew Proverbs*, Society of Biblical Literature: Dissertation Series, Scholars Press, Atlanta, (n.d.).
33. Eskenazi TC & Richards KH, *Second Temple Studies: 2 Temples and Community in the Persian Period*, JSOT Press, Sheffield, England, 1994, pp. 226-229.
34. Ibid. p.223.
35. Camp C, *Wisdom and the Feminine in the Book of Proverbs*, Bible and Literature, Volume 11, Almond Press, Sheffield, 1985, p.199.
36. Eskenazi TC & Richards KH, *Second Temple Studies: 2 Temples and Community in the Persian Period*, JSOT Press, Sheffield, England, 1994, pp.220-221.
37. Yee GA, *The Foreign Women in Proverbs 1-9*, Journal for the Study of Old Testament, Volume 43, 1989, pp.53-68.
38. Snijders LA, *The Meaning of 'Zar' in the Old Testament*, Old Testament Studies, Volume 10, 1954, p.67, also *see*: Botterweck GJ & Ringgren H (ed), *Theological Dictionary of the Old Testament*.
39. Eskenazi TC & Richards KH, *Second Temple Studies: 2 Temples and Community in the Persian Period*, JSOT Press, Sheffield, England, 1994, p.230.
40. Camp C, *Wisdom and the Feminine in the Book of Proverbs*, Bible and Literature, Volume 11, Almond Press, Sheffield, 1985, pp. 269-270.

41. Eskenazi TC & Richards KH, *Second Temple Studies: 2 Temples and Community in the Persian Period*, JSOT Press, Sheffield, England, 1994, p.231.
42. Weinberg JP, *Demographische Notizien zur Geschichte der nachexilischen Gemeinde in Juda*, Klio, Volume 54, 1972, pp. 45-58. For an English reference to these passages *see*: Eskenazi TC & Richards KH, *Second Temple Studies: 2 Temples and Community in the Persian Period*, JSOT Press, Sheffield, England, 1994, p.231.
43. Ibid. p.231.
44. Williamson HGM, *The Concept of Israel in Transition*, in Clements RE, *The World of Ancient Israel: Sociological, Anthropological and Political Perspectives*, Cambridge University, Cambridge, p.155.
45. Smith M, *Palestinian Parties and Politics that Shaped the Old Testament*, SCM Press, London, 1987, pp. 81-82.
46. Davies WD, Finkelstein L, *The Cambridge History of Judaism: The Persian Period*, Cambridge University Press, Cambridge, 1984, pp. 330-331.
47. Hoglund KG, *The Achaemenid Context*, in Davies PR, *Second Temple Studies,* Journal for the Study of Old Testament, Series 117, JSOT Press, Sheffield, 1991, p.67.
48. Merton RK, *Intermarriage and the Social Structure: Fact and Theory*, Issue 9 Psychiatry, 1941, p.362.
49. Ibid. pp. 65-66.
50. Washington HC, *The Strange Woman*, in Eskenazi TC & Richards KH, *Second Temple Studies: 2 Temples and Community in the Persian Period*, JSOT Press, Sheffield, England, 1994, pp. 217-242.
51. Camp C, *Wisdom and the Feminine in the Book of Proverbs*, Bible and Literature, Volume 11, Almond Press, Sheffield, 1985, p.251.
52. Washington HC, *The Strange Woman*, in Eskenazi TC & Richards KH, *Second Temple Studies: 2 Temples and Community in the Persian Period*, JSOT Press, Sheffield, England, 1994, p.240.
53. Hoglund K, *Achaemenid Imperial Administration in Syria-Palestine and the Missions of Ezra and Nehemiah*, (PhD Dissertation) Duke University, 1989.
54. Batten L, *Ezra and Nehemiah*, T&T Clark, Edinburg, 1980, p.331.
55. Williamson HGM, *Ezra and Nehemiah*, (Old Testament Guides), Sheffield Academic Press, England 1987, pp.130-132.
56. Merton RK, *Intermarriage and the Social Structure: Fact and Theory*, Issue 9 Psychiatry, 1941, pp.360 –370.

3

A CRITIQUE OF EZRA AND NEHEMIAH'S REMEDY FOR THE MARRIAGE CRISIS

INTRODUCTION

Watson and Hauser categorize the texts of Ezra and Nehemiah (Ezra 9-10 and Nehemiah 13) as narrative genre.[1] According to Culler, 'literary and cultural theory, have increasingly claimed cultural centrality for narrative. Narratives are the main way we make sense of things, whether in thinking of our lives in progression leading somewhere or in telling ourselves what is happening in the world.'[2] Scientific explanation makes sense of things by placing them under laws - *i.e.* whenever *a* and *b* obtain, *c* will occur. However, life does not generally follow this pattern, it follows not a scientific logic of cause and effect but the logic of story (narratives), where to understand is to conceive of how one thing leads to another, how something might have come about: how Ezra and Nehemiah ended up compelling a divorce on the men who took foreign women to be their wives.

The theory of narrative has been an active branch of literary theory, and literary study relies on theory of narrative structure, on notions of plot, of different kinds of narrators, of narrative techniques.[3] The 'poetics of narrative' attempts to understand the components of narrative and analyzes how particular narratives achieve their effects. Narratives also have the function, as theorists have emphasized, of teaching us about the world, showing us how it works, enabling us - through the devices of focalization - to see things from other vantage points, and to understand other motives (*e.g. divorce* as an ethical pragmatism) that in general are opaque to us. Even, when narratives are about people with wicked actions, they can solace us; they suggest a more comprehensible and thus, a more manageable human race. They give us the illusion of perspicacity and of power and show how aspirations are tamed and desires adjusted to social reality.[4] In this book I use the method of rhetorical criticism to provide a critique of various narrative texts pertaining to the content of discussion.

RHETORICAL CRITICISM ANALYSIS OF EZRA 9:1-10:44

Rhetorical Unit/s

The greater rhetorical unit is the problem of mixed marriages in Ezra 9:1–10:44. In these two chapters we encounter the crisis of mixed marriages, which was brought to the attention of Ezra.

First Rhetorical Unit: Ezra 9: 1-5 A Complaint Laid

The plaintiff or the party who brought the matter to the attention of Ezra, were the officials (9:1). According to Brockington, these were leading Jews, heads of father's houses.[5] They were probably those who had returned from exile, as it is they in whom the Chronicler's interest is centered and it was returning exiles that were accused of committing the offence (9:4, 10:6).

The Complaint: Exogamous Marriages

The first argumentative rhetorical unit begins with the narration of a complaint (9:1-2), which lays the exigence for the first argument, whose proposition centers on the people of Israel, the priests and the Levites not separating themselves from the people of the land by taking some of the daughters of the land to be wives for themselves and their sons. A digression ensues, amplifying this theme in 9:12, referring to the commandment of Yahweh through the servants and the prophets, that they should not give their daughters to the foreign sons, neither take foreign daughters for their sons, neither should they seek their peace or prosperity, that they may be strong and eat the good of the land, and leave it for an inheritance to their children.

These relationships between Judean men and the 'Strange Woman' were forbidden according to the law. However, in the post-exilic community they posed economic problems. Due to the land tenure and cultic membership being linked to genealogical lineage, the prospect of exogamous marriages brought the danger of outside encroachment upon the land holdings of the Judean congregation.[6] As within the patrilineal land tenure system women, *i.e.* the 'Strange Woman' was capable of inheriting and disposing property.

According to Brockington, since the mixed-marriage problem arose out of a complaint, it cannot be claimed that the marriage problem was one of the chief things for which Ezra returned.[7] It could have arisen out of a situation that needed the restructuring of that society, supporting Hoglund's theory that in order for the Persians to facilitate ease of identification for administration and taxation, there had to be an enforced guarded ethnic identity among the returning community, to whom they entrusted regions of the imperial domain.

According to Exodus 34:16 and Deuteronomy 7:1-3, the taking of foreign women to be their wives was contrary to the law. It jeopardized the purity of the 'holy race' and the institution of family; the true community had now been mixed with the people of the land. The gravity of the situation is expressed through the use of the adjective 'holy', which according to Brockington is a reference to Deuteronomy 7:6.[8]

The Accused

Those that had committed the offence were the laymen, officials and the chief men. The officials and chief men seem to have been the foremost (9:2). In Ezekiel 23:6 and Jeremiah 51:23 the *chief men* are spoken along with governors or satraps. However, in the texts of Ezra it is evidently used as a general word for *leaders*. They were the leaders of society. This shows the seriousness of the matter.

Ezra's Reaction

Reaction 1: Ezra on hearing about the current state of the community rent is garments and mantle. The renting of his clothing was a common act of distress (2 Samuel 13:19) and mourning (Genesis 37:34).

Reaction 2: 'pulled hair' - In this context the Chronicler associated the actions of pulling of hair as an act of grief. However, in Nehemiah

13:25 and Isaiah 50:6 it is an act of violence. There is evidence however, that baldness was a sign of grief and mourning (Leviticus 21:5, Deuteronomy 14:1), thus justifying Ezra's reaction to the complaint.

Reaction 3: 'sat appalled' - It was a common thing to sit or squat for a length of time when engaged in some such solemn act.[9] This act of Ezra is comparable in some ways with the acted prophecies of the Prophets, *cf.* Isaiah 20. Ezra's solitary act became a corporate act of contrition. The act of Ezra can be compared to the way in which the supporters railed around Moses after the golden calf incident in Exodus 32:26.

Second Rhetorical Unit: Ezra 9:6-15 Ezra's Prayer

The second argumentative rhetorical unit is a ring composition, which begins and ends with the proposition of Ezra's prayer, governing the rest of the discussion. The major topic addressed is the element of repentance for disobedience of the commandment from Yahweh. Ezra can be seen as the legal representative of the people, presenting their case before the 'Judge' - Yahweh in the form of a prayer.

Ezra States the Case and Pleads Guilty of Disobedience to the Commandment of Yahweh (9:6-10)

The change of person from first singular in *6a* to first plural in *6b* can be envisaged as Ezra's consciousness that he stands in a unique position, privileged to speak to God and therefore beginning on an intensely personal note.[10] However, at the same time he identifies himself with the community and passing through a vicarious experience on their behalf.

Ezra (9:6-10) acknowledges in his prayer that they have been in great guilt and due to the consequences of their iniquities they have suffered at the hands of the kings of the land (*i.e.* Assyrian - Nehemiah 9:32, Babylonian and Persian - Nehemiah 9:37). However, for a brief moment (*8a*), referring to the period of restoration following the Decree of Cyrus, Yahweh has shown favour to His people.

He has left them as the '*remnant*'. The word '*remnant*' used in this text does not refer to those left over, but rather those who have escaped (*see* also 9:14), where two words are used, the one meaning remnant - *i.e.* left over, and the other word used in 9:8 meaning those who escaped (*see* 9:15): it is the returned exiles who are meant by both words - *i.e.* they have escaped out of their exile and they are what remain of the Israelite people (Nehemiah 1:2).

According to the narration of the prayer of Ezra, we note an important phrase contributing to Washington's theory to the sociology of the mixed marriage crisis in the post-exilic Judean community. Ezra prays that Yahweh has blessed the remnant with a '*secure hold*'- literally translated as a '*nail*' or '*tent peg*' (9:8). It is probably the figure of the tent peg that the Chronicler has in mind, since the peg would be used to pin down the nomad's tent and give security. According to Brockington, one might also see in it a sense of tenure, of the right to be there, a right to possess the land, a sense of belonging, *i.e.* a right to place their peg in the land.[11] The implication is that restoration had proceeded so far that the people, could feel settled and secure. This could also be a reference to the endorsement from the Persian Empire, to those who took membership in the re-established *Bürger-Tempel-Gemeinde* as an act of securing their legal right to land.

According to Ezra (9:9), Yahweh has not forsaken them, but has extended His steadfast love before the kings of Persia, to grant them some reviving to set up the house of Yahweh. The term '*reviving*' can be understood using Hoglunds theory of land allotment to refer to *land* being given by the Persian kings to the returning community.

Acknowledges the Commandment (9:11-12)

Following the plea of guilt, is the acknowledgement of the commandment given by the prophets. Batten traces this commandment back to the book of Deuteronomy: 'The land which you go in to possess (Deuteronomy 7:1) is a polluted land, by the pollution of the people of the land, by their abominations in that they have filled it from end to end with their uncleanness. And now you shall not give your daughters to their sons nor shall you take their daughters for your sons (Deuteronomy 7:3). And you shall not seek their peace and their good forever (Deuteronomy 23:7) in order that you may be strong and eat the good of the land and possess it for your sons forever.'[12]

The word *'abominations'* occurs in Deuteronomy 13 indicating practices of aliens/foreigners, which are forbidden to Israel. *'The good of the land'* in the sense of its best products occurs in Genesis 45:18-20. Nowhere in the Pentateuch is Palestine called a polluted land, contrary it is a land that is flowing with milk and honey. However, the idea of a polluted land is found in Leviticus 18:24-30, where the land is called unclean by reason of the abomination practiced by the peoples who preceded Israel in its occupation. The *'people of the land'* (*i.e.* 'foreigners') is characteristic of the Chronicler.

The citation is made up of Deuteronomic phrases patched together loosely and is cited as a divine command by the prophets (a commandment from Yahweh). Ezra is thought to have carried the law-book in his hand and could have been able to quote literally.[13] This particular precept which was so flagrantly disobeyed is quoted literally enough (against intermarriage), and the statement about the land is made to reinforce the danger of marital alliance. By marrying foreign women, the abominations, which have made the land unclean, will adhere to Israel (the remnant).[14] The land will fall into the hands of foreign women and offspring of abominations.

A Plea for Mercy (9:13-15)

The plea for mercy, though formally still addressed to God, is clearly intended as an exhortation to the people, and apply much more precisely than what as preceded to the immediate subject of anxiety: the joining in marriage with foreigners, jeopardized the purity of the holy race and threatened the economic stability of the Judean temple economy with the issue of the land allotment.[15] The punishment, which Israel had endured, was not due to the injustice of God, for the people had richly deserved their woes. The same conditions, which destroyed earlier Israel, were prevalent in the post-exilic period. If the guilt of Israel persisted, their life would be short. The future depended upon strict obedience to the law.[16]

According to Batten, this prayer was evidently intended to produce an effect upon the audience rather than upon God.[17] Ezra waited until a considerable congregation had assembled before he began to pray. The whole tenor of the prayers shows the desire to touch the heart of the guilty and to impel them to abandon the course of life, which seemed so evil. The rhetorical unit concluded with a direct appeal to God, and the use once again of the theme of a remnant.

Third Rhetorical Unit: Ezra 10:1-5 Covenant and Oath to Divorce Foreign Wives

The material relating to the forced divorce, *i.e.* 'putting away' of the foreign women reverts to the third person (as in Ezra 7). We can regard this as the Chronicler incorporating into the narrative another source. The parallels with Nehemiah, already noted several times, are carried a stage further, for Ezra's action here is closely parallel to that carried out by Nehemiah in Nehemiah 13:23-30.

Shechaniah Proposes Forced Divorce as a Method to Rectify the Social Crisis

In this rhetorical unit, Ezra's praying and loud weeping attracts a very large crowd (it was time of the evening sacrifice and Ezra was praying in the temple). Shechaniah 'answered' Ezra. In Hebrew the word 'answer' is idiomatical to introduce a statement made, not as a reply to a spoken word, but with reference to an act upon which the answer is a comment.[18] Shechaniah admits that Israel has done wrong and proposes that the offenders shall be put under oath to divorce their foreign wives and the children born from them.

In this third rhetorical unit we note that the zeal for establishing the true community is not confined to Ezra and the priestly ranks only. Shechaniah, apparently a layman acknowledges guilt on behalf of the community and willingness to take appropriate action.[19] According to Brockington, Shechaniah seems to be acting as a clear-minded spokesman of those who were zealous for the purity of race.[20] The appropriate action according to 10:3 is *'to put away all these wives and children.'* Literally translated to *'put away'* or *'to eject'*, occurs only here and in verse 19 as a verb for divorcing for which the usual verb is one meaning *'send away'* (Deuteronomy 24:1).[21]

In 9:4 there gathered at the beginning 'all who trembled at the words of the God of Israel'. The rendering cited would make them according to Batten, a party to the proposed plan, and would put the proposal for forced divorce into the mouth of Ezra.[22] Ezra in his prayer had suggested no drastic remedy. In fact it seems as though he left it entirely to others to advise the heroic course to be followed.

Ezra Sanctions the Proposal

While the law forbade mixed marriages, it did not, unless by inference provide for their dissolution.[23] Was divorce forced? The plan according to Brockington, was Shechaniah's plan for the rectification of the problem, as there was no law ordering a divorce in such cases. However, Ezra sanctioned the plan of rectification (10:4-5).[24]

A Covenant was made by the Leaders to Implement the Proposal

The covenant was made and the leading priests and Levites and all Israel took the oath that they would forcefully divorce their foreign wives and children. This could be translated according to Brockington as 'the leaders' ('officials' in 9:2) of the priests, of the Levites and of all Israel took the covenant.[25] This seems preferable and would then be a proper move by Ezra because (a) some of the leaders themselves were involved in marriage with foreign women and (b) only through these could the rank and file be reached.

Ezra accepted Shechaniah's plan, the leaders made a covenant to implement the plan and a decree was issued ordering all Israel to convene within three days under penalty of confiscation of land and ex-communication.

Fourth Rhetorical Unit: Ezra 10:6-8 An Assembly Summoned

Ezra and his Temporary Lodging

Ezra's prayer had been offered at the time of evening sacrifice (9:5). In this rhetorical unit we now approach nightfall and are told of Ezra's temporary lodging place. His abstinence from food and water signifies fasting, which enters largely into the religious life of the people of this period.[26]

The Consequences of the Failure to Attending the Assembly

According to rhetorical unit three, an assembly was to be summoned within three days. This was to be a general assembly to carry out the agreement subscribed by the oath of the leaders. The three days signifies the narrow bounds of the new community. Ezra himself was much in the background (10:8). He was impelling the rulers to act.[27] A severe penalty was to be imposed upon those who did not comply with the edict. The punishment would be two-fold, namely :—

(a) All his property would be confiscated, and,
(b) he should be separated from the assembly of the captivity (*i.e.* ex-communicated).

According to the hypothesis of Washington, an ulterior motive to the propagation of the actions that were deemed necessary by the officials and elders was the fear that Judean property will fall under the control of foreign families, *via* relationships and eventual marriages to women outside the community. In an analysis of the actions of this commission, they identified and prosecuted those who had married outside the community (10:16). Thus, we can understand that the failure to submit to these proceedings (*i.e.* the assembly 10:9), included expulsion from the temple assembly and the confiscation of the property. Thus, counteracting the possibility of land falling into the hands of the foreign families and the foreign women.

The authority for the edict, which undertook to punish heavily those who disobeyed it, was not that of Ezra, but of the oligarchy, 'the elders and the leaders' (10:8).[28] In the whole passage, the emphasis is upon the single expression, *'the matter is upon you'*. There is no hint of any authority vested in Ezra. However, he does administer the oath that binds the leaders to execute the plan of Shechaniah.

Fifth Rhetorical Unit: Ezra 10:9-15

Assembly Held and Arrangements made to handle the Problem

The Attendance at the Assembly

The proclamation was issued in Judah and Jerusalem, according to rhetorical unit four. It appears that the threat in verse 8 was effective, as the response is declared to be general, all the people gathered without any exception.[29] The congregation gathered in the *plaza*, an open space before the water gate (Nehemiah 3:26, 8:1), a favourite place for assemblies. Batten argued that the number of people was not as great as verse *9a* would have implied, for there was not a large place to accommodate the congregation.[30]

The Reason for the Assembly

Ezra the *priest*, previously called 'the scribe' (7:11, 7:21 and Nehemiah 12:26), is now performing duties that are not scribal but priestly. And so that title is substituted with the title 'priest'. Ezra states that the reason for the summoning of the assembly is because they have transgressed against the law and married foreign women. They have *'added/increased the guilt of Israel'*. The phrase indicates that by the violation of the law, the present generation was increasing the already large record of national sin.

The Plan of Action

The author of this narration seems to have drawn form the appeal made to Achan in Joshua 7:18, where as a parallel we have 'give glory'. The idea in this text may be to praise God (*i.e.* do His will). Praise/confession was due to God because the offenders were brought to a state of amendment.[31] There is a double demand of action required:

(a) separate yourselves from the nations of the land, and
(b) separate yourselves from the foreign women.

These actions are in agreement with the plan proposed by Shechaniah and sanctioned by Ezra. The Israelites were called upon to cut off all association with the foreigners.

Agreement and Disagreement to the Plan of Action

The congregation, which gathered in the assembly were ready, to meet the demands (*i.e.* compelling a divorce). However, the conditions made it impossible (a) there were too many cases, (b) the unpredictable conditions of the weather. It was a period of winter rains, called 'the former rains' in Deuteronomy 11:14. Ezra's zeal was not dependent upon the weather, but that the number who had married foreigners was relatively very large. Verse 14 contains the counter-proposal of the people. We may render the text as:—

> 'let now our leaders stand for the whole assembly, and let all who are in our cities that have married foreign women come at appointed times, and with the elders of each city and its judges...'

The counter-proposal follows three steps, namely:—

(a) The leaders should take charge of the business for the whole assembly;
(b) To this tribunal all transgressors should come at appointed times (*cf.* Nehemiah 10:35), and
(c) The guilty should appear with the local elders and judges.

The function of the local officers is left to conjecture, it is natural to suppose, that their office was to see that the decrees of the tribunal were carried out. In considering the procedure of a divorce and the issuing of a '*get*' certificate of divorce, we can understand why it was necessary to meet before a judge. It appears that the divorce court sat in Jerus, and that all proceedings took place here.[32]

In verse 16 we find a fragment and a discovery of opposition to the divorce. Four men, namely:—

(a) Jonathan the son of Asahel,
(b) Josiah the son of Tikvah,
(c) Meshullam, and
(d) Shabbethai the Levite.

According to Batten, these four men stood in opposition to the plan of action.[33] In the light of Brockington's analysis, we are not told of why the four men were in opposition. But it may be that the opposition was directed only at the method adopted and not at the basic measure.[34]

Sixth Rhetorical Unit: Ezra 10:16-17A Three Month Task

The sixth rhetorical unit begins with an agreement and endorsement of the congregation present at the assembly to carry out the plan for divorce. Ezra selects a divorce tribunal to deal with the issue at hand. Verse 16 *'Ezra ...selected men'* the adoption of the Greek text (LXX) according to Brockington is clearly desirable since the Hebrew is ungrammatical and could only be rendered,[35] *'And Ezra the Priest, men who were heads of houses, were separated....'* These men of the divorce tribunal were designated by name. However, the Chronicler does not list their names in this text. Brockington suggested that the list appeared in Ezra's memoirs, but the Chronicler chose not to use it.[36] The question in this rhetorical unit is how many and whom did he choose? He may have followed tradition and chosen 12, the representative tribal number.

'The heads of the fathers' are the clan leaders called *'our leaders'* by the people in verse 14. The tribunal was charged with executive rather than judicial functions. The tenth month corresponds with December-January. Some ancient texts have the twelfth month, but that would make the session of the court one month instead of three, and it would have convened two and one-third months after the assembly, instead of ten days.[37] This rhetorical unit ends with a list of names of the offenders being established by the first day of the first month.

Seventh Rhetorical Unit: Ezra 10: 18-44 Lists of Offenders: Priests, Levites and Laymen

The final rhetorical unit is a list of the offenders that married foreign women. In the list that follows, the four priestly families, Joshua the son of Jozadak and his brethren, Immer, Harim, and Pashhur, correspond with those in 2:36-39, except that the first is differently designated, namely Jedaiah of the house of Joshua. The Levites are not divided into families. There are eleven lay families mentioned (whereas in 2:3-20 there are seventeen), but four of the eleven do not occur in Ezra 2, namely, Harim, Binnui, Nebo and the second Bani. Twenty-one of the names occur twice or more in the list. This reduces the number of different names in the list to seventy-nine, nineteen of which occur only in this list.

A guilt offering was required by the men that trespassed against the law. According to Leviticus 5:14-19, the ram was compensation for a guilt offering where sin was committed unwittingly. From a religious perspective defilement is not merely a symbol of something in contradiction - *i.e.* the balance on which ideas of virtue and sin are weighed, but the basic condition of all reality.[38] There is probably no need to press this point and think that the people did not know that they were contravening the law. It should be assumed that although it is not mentioned in the rest of the list, all the guilty men would be called upon to make the same sacrifice.[39] The rhetorical unit ends in verse 44. In a very few words the result of Ezra's marriage reform is set out. The men guilty of marrying the foreign women forcefully divorced their wives and children.

Relational Posture of the Rhetorical Unit/s

This is the most theoretically complex step in the analysis, as many different aspects of the text can be discussed and evaluated. In this book, I explore the relationship of modality and deixis to the network of intentions (of texts, author and reader), which become apart of the background/context of the reading.

Modalities

Modalities[40] control the presentation, that is, the relationship asserted within the argument concerning divorce. Modalities modify the reality, the certainty, or the importance of the argument.[41] They operate not only within the text's intentionality, but in the audience as well. For specific forms of modalities to function in this interaction, there must be a set of conditions provided by the background/context, this being determined by natural possibilities (author's and readers ability/skill in communication), norms, social values and desires, and the communicants' beliefs and knowledge.[42] In the greater rhetorical unit of the mixed marriage crisis in the texts of Ezra, I find two major modals among the major argumentative units: Cognitional and volitional modes.

Cognitional Modal

In the cognitional[43] modal, the author and audience share (a) a call status and (b) a common commitment to known traditions. In the call status the author and the audience acknowledges that they are the 'remnant' (9:8) of Israel, they are the 'holy seed/race' (9:2) and they are the 'true community' (9:1) that has returned from exile to re-establish itself. The author shares a history with the audience of the sufferings in exile and now given the opportunity to live as a blessed remnant of God, there has to be a social transformation from their past guilt, and sinful state to a new life in Yahweh as the holy remnant.

The common commitment to known tradition is firstly the law, which both the audience and the author share (9:11-12). The precept of the prophets is found in Deuteronomy 7, *i.e.* the law forbidding the marriage to foreigners, a call for the separation from the people of the land and their abominations.

There is also a common understanding between the author and the audience to the polemic against the foreign women in the wisdom literature and the post-exilic Judean community in accordance to the land tenure system and the threat that these foreign relationships posed to the economic stability of the Judean temple economy (Proverbs 1-9).

Volitional Modal

Within the volitional[44] modal we see a give and take in discussion of topics made both within an atmosphere of independence of judgement, confession, exhortation, authoritative command/sanction and shame. The location of certain codes, postures, judgements, etc. against a background of context.

In the second rhetorical unit of Ezra's prayer, we find elements of exhortation for the mercy of God (9:7-10), an exhortation to the audience that they are the holy remnant (9:8). Confession is made for disobeying the commandment and shame at the consequences of their actions (9:10-14), a plea for God's mercy and a request for a solution to the problem. At the ending of the prayer, Batten notes an intentional posture, which is used by Ezra although he is still in conversation with God (9:13-14). The intention at the ending of the prayer is a rectification needed from the audience to stipulate some form of action, which will rectify the shame.[45]

In this posture or coded form, Ezra addresses the audience of the mercy that God has shown to them in exile and as returnees from exile. Now it is upon them, to rectify the sin, which they have committed and make confession to the God that has been merciful to them or fall into his hands of judgement (*i.e.* wrath and retribution). The sanctioning of the proposed plan to divorce the foreign wives is an authoritative command by Ezra (10:3-4). However, it was proposed by a spokesman of the people and accepted by the people (10:2). The acceptance of the proposal by the people at the assembly to divorce their foreign wives is met by a counter-proposal to the procedure of divorce (10:13-14). The sanction to divorce their wives is taken as authoritative from Ezra and the commission and implemented as authoritative on the foreign wives by their husbands (10:44). Using the volitional modal, we can clearly note a compromising element/ factor in these argumentative rhetorical units.

Deixis

Deixis orients the content of a sentence in relationship to time, place and personal participants. Indexical expressions are used to construct contexts of utterances and references, relating both what is said and the reader of what is written to a cultural, social and historical context in which people interact through language reflecting social roles, perceptions and positions. The basic function of deixis is 'to relate the actors and concerns referred in the text to the spatiotemporal...here-and-now of the context of the utterance that is not just a production, but also of the performance'.[46]

Personal Deixis

The personal deixis includes the use of person and demonstrative pronouns, as well as the use of personal names and perhaps substantives. In the first rhetorical unit (9:1-5), when the complaint is being launched, we have a reference to *'the people of Israel'* (9:1) that had committed the offence as *'they'* (9:2). We know that there are certain people in the community that had committed the offence and transgressed against the law. The word *'they'* is an exclusive term. The '*plantiff*' and *'I'* (Ezra) are set in distinction from *'they'*.

In the second rhetorical unit (9:6-15), in the prayer of Ezra, Ezra starts with a personal reference *'I'* (9:6). He stands before God for the iniquities of his people. However, (in 9:6) we are introduced to Ezra praying as *'our'* iniquities. Literally, it would mean that Ezra is part of the guilty (inclusive). To justify the change from first singular in *6a* to first plural in *6b*, Brockington suggested that Ezra's prayer is the *prayer of an accused*, he is not guilty but he shares the sin of the community.[47] The words *'I'*, *'our'* and *'we'* are now used as inclusive terms. In the third rhetorical unit we are introduced to the collective terms of *'we'* and *'us'* referring to the offenders. In this rhetorical unit we note the return to the use of exclusive terms such as *'they'* (9:5) and *'your'* (9:4).

In the first rhetorical unit the readership is addressed as *'the people of Israel and ....'* (9:1), but once the second rhetorical unit begins the readership is addressed as the *'remnant'* (9:8). The remnant refers to a greater social designation in the life of Israel to those that had escaped and now returned from exile. The remnant refers to the true community. In the context of personal deixis, one should also note the use of (a) proper names, (b) social groups, (c) types and (d) places:

(a) Proper Names	
Ezra : Priest and Scribe	10:6
Foreign wives:	
Canaanites,Hittites, Perizzites, Jebusites, Ammonites, Moabites, Egyptians, Amorites	9:1
Shechaniah son of Jehiel:	
Laymen and spokesman of the offenders,	
Proposer of action: forced divorce	10:2
Jehohanan son of Eliashin	
With whom Ezra temporary lodged	10:6
Jonathan son of Asahel	10:15
Jahzeiah son of Tikvah	
Meshulam	
Shabbethai	
Opposition to the method employed by Ezra and the commission	
A list of offenders (*see* p. 123)	10:18-44
(b) Social Groups	
Laymen : The people of Israel	9:1
Priests	9:1

(Contd.)

Levites	9:1
Officials	9:2
Chiefmen	9:2
Judges	10:14
Tribes : Judah and Benjamin	10:9
Kings of Persia	9:9
(c) Types	
People of the land: foreign women	9:1
Holy race	9:2
Returned exiles	9:4
Remnant	9:8
Bondmen	9:9
Heads of fathers houses: social leaders	10:16
(d) Places	
Persia	9:9
Judea	9:9
Jerusalem	9:9
Plaza: The assembly place – an open square	10:9

Through these groupings, the text directs the attention of the reader to some intentional content, that is, through their representational aspects. When the Chronicler/author refers to groups, individuals, types or places, certain implications are being made. However, these implications are highly contextual (on the part of the text, author and audience).

Intonational Deixis

Intonational deixis serves to express emotion to some greater or lesser degree, but more importantly serves as an evaluative attitude on the part of the speaker/author toward a given social understanding held with respect to the given attributes.[48]

Author, Mix Marriages and the Polemic against the Foreign Women

In 9:1 and 9:2 we note the emotion of the author expressed towards the foreign wives and the Judean men. The author refers to the foreign wives as *'the people of the land with their abominations'*, which stands in contrast to the Judean men as *'the holy race'*. *'Abominations'* stands in contrast to *'holy'*, thus expressing the author's attitude to the acceptance of the polemic against the foreign women. He provokes the marriage to the foreign women, motivating that the holy race will become impure. This can be explained with reference to 9:14, where inter-marrying with the foreign women, will result in Israel inheriting their abominations.

In the following verse: *'...that you may be strong, and eat the good of the land and leave if for an inheritance to your children forever'* (9:12), illustrates Merton's exchange theory of what advantages did the foreign women gain by marrying outside their social boundaries.[49] We can argue that the foreign women married the Israelites with the intention to gain access to the land. Failure to heed to the law will imply that the land will go to the foreign families and not the 'remnant'. This land according to the author is divine land given to the remnant by God (9:8).

No matter what theory one would accept, there is clearly negativity (9:6), remorse (9:7) and anger (9:3) expressed by the author towards the inter-marriage with the foreign women. The descriptive terms *'faithlessness'* (9:2) *'appalled'* (9:4) and *'ashamed'* (9:5) express the disappointment of the author to the 'remnant' in transgressing against the prohibition. In 10:3 *'all these wives and their children'*, the author sets a distinction and exclusion of the foreign women and their children by using the terms *'these'* and *'their'*. He excludes them from the community but maintains the right of the Judean men to whom these women were married. Terms such as *'holy seed'* clearly illustrate a sense of group xenophobia.[50]

Author on Divorce

In 10:12, *'Then all the assembly answered in a loud voice'*, the question that arises is why does the author use the phrase *'in a loud voice'*? Batten suggested that the phrase should be explained using the Hebrew usage in 2 Chronicles 15:14 and 20:19, where the author uses the Hebrew phrase to express *earnestness*.[51]

The actions of Ezra, sanctioning Shechaniah's proposal for forced divorce should not be judged from the highest standards of our day, but from the ethical conceptions of his own time and people. Divorce was a very simple process in Israel, and there was no stigma attached to it. A public hearing was not necessary, and no official sanction was required. A man who wanted to divorce his wife, for any cause, had only to give her a bill of divorce and send her away. The possible hardships to the foreign women are easily exaggerated from sentimental considerations, but such an idea would hardly enter the mind of author, Ezra or his contemporaries.

Therefore, through an analysis of the phrase, *'loud voice'*, it clearly illustrates that the author considered the process of divorce socially acceptable and socially viable, hence, showed no remorse in the implementation of the method.

Spatial Deixis

Spatial deixis is used with respect to geographical names and spaces.[52] In rhetorical unit 1, the narrative commences with Ezra's reformation in Jerusalem (9:1). In 9:2, there is a reference to the Canaanites, Hittites, Perizzites, Jebusites, Ammonites, Moabites, Egyptians and the Amorites as being the people of the land, *i.e.* the foreign wives. In rhetorical unit 2, (9:6) Ezra is in the temple praying. In 9:9, there is a reference to the kings of Persia that grants protection to Judea and Jerusalem. In rhetorical unit 4, a proclamation is made throughout Judah and Jerusalem to all the returned exiles that they should meet in Jerusalem (10:7). In rhetorical unit 5, men of Judah and Benjamin assembled at Jerusalem (10:9). The narrative ends with a list of offenders from their respective cities (10:18-44).

Temporal Deixis

Temporal deixis is present in rhetorical unit 2. Where the tension between the current social state and the future fulfilment as the remnant is highlighted by the distinction from the *'days of the fathers'* (9:7) to *'this day'* (9:7). Set against cultural codes of what is believed, known and valued, the author devaluates the past experience of being in bondage with great guilt and their iniquities, evaluates the present state of the 'remnant' with the mixed marriage crisis, God's mercy and blessings of security, land and grace of being the remnant.

He then sets a background of the disobedience of the 'remnant', by transgressing against the law and intermarrying with the foreign women, to God's consummation of them, His wrath and leaving no remnant and escape (9:14). The author argues for the future existence of the 'remnant', as distinct from the past experiences *'the days of our fathers'* (9:7), and attempts to make manifest a new cultural code *'in this day'* (9:7). He compares God's blessing of a *'secure hold'* (*i.e.* land) to fulfilment of the law and divorcing the foreign women thereby leaving the *'secure hold'* as a future inheritance for their children.

Method of Argumentation

In general, we can assume that the intention of the author's argument centred on the purity of Israel and the consequences of failing to maintain its purity. In his argument we have two major factors that seek the attention of the audience, which fostered the proposed actions to force divorce. Firstly, the Deuteronomic legal basis for the action taken by Ezra in Ezra 9-10, and the fact that the Deuteronomic laws are being stretched to justify this action.[53] Secondly, the social meaning of this action in the context of the post-exilic community and its attempt to preserve its purity and/or maintain its economic holdings without threat of foreigners inheriting land.[54]

The failure to maintain this purity would heed the consequences of Israel as a remnant ceasing to exist, and land falling into the hands of foreign families. The author's argument intends on substantiating the economic and social disintegration of society. As a result, the relationships with foreign women were not economically and socially viable in the reconstruction of the society of the returning exiles.

A mutual basis, which develops further argumentation is formed in the introductory section (*i.e.* rhetorical unit 1), in which the 'call' status of the Israelites as a remnant and the need to separate from the people of the land is established, together with the complaint of transgressing against the law to foreign women (rhetorical fact). The author's stasis statement, a complaint being laid by the officials of the mixed marriage crisis resulting in a contamination of the holy race (9:2), helps to set up the argumentative units. This leads him to the proposition of the greater rhetorical unit (9:14), 'shall we break the commandments again and intermarry with the people who practice these abominations? Will you not be angry with us and consume us, so that there should not be any remnant, nor any escape?'

In order both to amplify the proposition and to set up the basis for the argument proposing the actions of forced divorce, the author inserts a lengthy digression of a *prayer of an accused* (in rhetorical unit 2).

Dissociative

In considering rhetorical unit 2: The prayer of Ezra, to be a source from Ezra's memoir, we note that the method of argumentation is dissociative. The author separates himself from the guilty community and stands before God as the accused for the community (9:7). Separation now allows him to define in negative terms the shame and guilt for the consequences of the community's transgressions against the law with relationships to the foreign women.

He uses this dissociative method to define the nature of the relationship that exists between Yahweh and the remnant (present and past). This technique of argumentation is used to pose an evaluation upon the actions of the audience (*i.e.* the community) through a mirror perspective. The audience listening to the prayer of Ezra is presented with an argumentation for social reform.

Rhetorical Reality

Appealing to a historical structure of rhetorical reality, the author now sets up his position within the framework of Israel's historical background. Due to their past guilt and sins they were given into the hands of the kings of Persia, Babylon and Assyria, to the sword, to captivity, to plundering and to utter shame (9:7). This was their retribution for transgressing against the words of Yahweh. However, presently Yahweh has shown grace and mercy to them. He has delivered them from exile, restored them as a remnant and granted them prosperity and blessings of a land they can possess (9:8). For this mercy and blessings, all Yahweh commanded was that they should not take the daughters of the land, for their abominations exceed their reputation and beauty. This serves to put the community equally responsible for their actions, as Ezra the Priest is responsible before

Yahweh. This strategy limits the role of the audience to passive recipients, for which no one can boast or think of them as being the remnant unless they take some form of action to rectify their guilt.

He now picks up where he left off. He and the audience are now in a position where they are aware of the paradigm of the situation and have been introduced to the basis upon which the argument is founded. He can now turn to the question of the attitude of the audience (9:15 'Behold, we are before thee in our guilt, for none can stand before thee because of our guilt'). The irony of Ezra's actions in 10:1 'confessing, weeping and casting himself down before the house of God, is intended to shame the guilty community that gathered around him. This seems to have worked since the people that gathered around Ezra began to weep bitterly (10:1).

So admonished, they are now in position to see their faults, and Ezra can turn to them and appeal for some forms of social transformation to rectify the situation. In the third rhetorical unit, the author's direction is to allow the community, once they understand the basic message the author is attempting to communicate, to judge and act for themselves. At no point in this rhetorical unit or the previous units does he propose a form of action, but through his prayer and actions, he allows them to judge what is practical and helpful.

The major heading in the third rhetorical unit is the proposed action of compelling a 'divorce'. The audience is now an active recipient. A new logical reciprocity is formed: 'We have broken faith with our God and have married foreign women...but even now there is still hope for Israel in spite of this' (10:2). The following issue is handled by means of establishing a maxim by some universal acceptance of hope. Thus, justifying the proposed actions based on the concept of the structure of reality. In 10:3 the basic premise is outlined: 'let us make a covenant to put away all these wives and their children'. Referring back to the call status of the community, he appeals to the structure of reality in this argument supporting the polemic against the foreign women - *i.e.* an exclusive terminology *'they'* emphasizing that *'they'* are not part of the remnant.

In the final argumentative structure to be discussed here, there is a change of strategy (the implications of which we will explore next), for in this argument there is a counter-proposal and an opposition. The audience agrees on the compelling to divorce the foreign wives

(10:12) but disagrees on the method of impelling the compulsion due to the constraints of the weather and the number of offenders. It was proposed and accepted that the officials stand as representatives of the people to implement the compelling of divorce. However, four others met this in opposition.

Shifts in Argumentative Situation

The shifts evidenced in the argumentative situation throughout the performance of the narrative are now clarified by the previous discussion. In the first major argumentative unit, a complaint is laid of the transgression against the law and the current state of the community (9:1-5).

In the second rhetorical unit, there is a shift from the plaintiff to Ezra (9:6-15). Ezra is seeking to re-establish the community as being the remnant of God. He shows the people a historical significance of the past sin and guilt and the retribution it has yielded the community (9:7). He then shifts to the present state of the community and the mercy that Yahweh has granted them (9:8). He then shifts to a future perspective of the continuation of their sin, which will result in the extinction of the remnant (9:14) and the loosing of the land. He then shifts back to the present state leaving the decision for social transformation in the hands of his audience (9:15) and the ability to leave an inheritance for their children (9:12).

Then comes a major shift between the first and second argumentative units. It is only when Ezra feels that he has successfully made the audience aware of their consequences that we then have an active response from the audience proposing a method to counteract the problem (10:1-5).

Another major shift is made in rhetorical unit 5. Here Ezra finds himself and the audience finally in the position to address the issue at hand, *i.e.* the social transformation of the community to re-establish itself as the true 'remnant' and secure the land within the holdings of the remnant (10:9-15). This is the culmination of the previous matters discussed. Ezra achieves this climax, a method socially acceptable to implement social transformation to rectify society's disparagement.

We are then introduced to a shift in the argumentation from Ezra proposing a method of divorce, to the audience's counter-proposal

(10:13). The audience appealing to the argument based on the proposition of reality finds the proposed implementation impossible to be done in one day. However, the method of forced divorce is accepted (10:12). The counter-proposal is met with a suggestion, which is accepted by Ezra. However, four men stood in opposition to the procedure (10:15). This opposition was probably directed at the method adopted and not at the basic measure.[55] The author then shifted to the argumentation of the counter-proposal being accepted and implemented to the formation of a divorce tribunal (10:16). The argument for social change ends with a success of implementation (10:44).

Classification of Argument

We are now in a position to assess the greater rhetorical intention of the mixed marriage crisis. All the methodological approaches so far, have led us to the point, where now we can most effectively classify the genre/function of the various parts of the larger rhetorical unit.

Narrative Analysis

Alter identifies the texts of Ezra as narrative.[56] In order for us to account adequately for the nature of the discourse of the mixed marriage crisis in the Post-Exilic Judean community (Ezra 9-10), it is situated and interpreted in terms of its function in the narrative as a whole. An analysis of the narrative will be performed using Rimmon-Kenan's distinction between (a) Story, (b) Text, and (c) Narration.[57]

Narrative Theory as Story

In considering narrative theory as story Rimmon-Kenan makes a distinction between *events* and *characters*.[58]

Events in the Story

In the story of the mixed marriage crisis in the post-exilic Judean community we have several events within the larger rhetorical unit. The first event is the complaint being laid by the officials (9:1-5).

The second event is the public prayer of Ezra (9:6-15). The third event is the proposed plan of action (10:2-3). The fourth event is the covenant and oath to divorce the foreign wives (10:4-5). The fifth event is the summoning of an assembly (10:6-8). The sixth event is the holding of the assembly and the arrangements made to implement the proposal (10:9-15). The seventh event is the selection of the tribunal council and the three-month task (10:16-17). And finally, the eighth event is the compilation of the list of offenders (10:18-44).

Characters in the Story

With consideration of the definition of characters on story level, Rimmon-Kenan makes a distinction between *flat* and *round characters.*[59] *Flat Characters* have only one trait, quality, or idea attached to them. *Round Characters* are more complex and involves having more than one quality and developing in the course of action.

Characters	*Flat/Round*
Ezra : Priest and Scribe	Round
Foreign wives:	
Canaanites, Hittites, Perizzites, Jebusites,	
Ammonites, Moabites, Egyptians, Amorites	Round
Shechaniah son of Jehiel:	
Laymen and spokesman of the offenders,	
Proposer of action: forced divorce	Round
Jehohanan son of Eliashin	
With whom Ezra temporary lodged	Flat
Jonathan son of Asahel	
Jahzeiah son of Tikvah	
Meshulam	
Shabbethai	
Opposition to the method employed by Ezra and	
the commission	Flat
A list of offenders (see p. 123)	Flat
The Accused:	Round
Laymen : The people of Israel	
Priests	

(Contd.)

Levites	
Chiefmen	
The Plaintiff:	Round
Officials	
Judges	Flat
Tribes: Judah and Benjamin	Round
Kings of Persia	Flat

Narrative Theory as Text

In accounting for narrative theory as text, Rimmon-Kenan makes a distinction between (i) time, (ii) characterization, and (iii) focalization.[60]

Time

Time concerns the textual arrangement of the event component of the story in the text. Although, time is inescapably linear as we read the narrative text, a comparison between text time and conventional story time reveals that a hypothetical norm of complete correspondence between the two is only rarely realized. Genette explains these discordances through comparing *order, duration and frequency* of events in the text.[61]

Order of Events

Order specifies the analeptic (or 'flashback') and proleptic (or 'foreshadowing') relations between the story and text-time. Examples in Ezra 9-10 can be found in the analeptic references by Ezra to their past retribution of Israel (9:7) and in the foreshadowing of Yahweh's consummation and anger leaving no remnant and escape (9:14) due to their iniquities in transgressing against the law.

Duration of Events

Duration specifies the difference between the length of time an event takes in the story and textual levels. Example, the reading of the narrative discourse of the mixed marriage crisis on the textual level is different from the actual story level. A brief summary of the response by the Jews with their counter-proposal (10:13) could have taken much longer than the time it takes the reader to read about it.

Day 1: 16th of the 9th Month

According to Batten, the narrative begins proceeding, the references to the depositing of the treasure in the temple, the sacrifices and the delivery of the edict (9:1).[62] The complaint is brought to the attention of Ezra. An entire day passes with Ezra mourning the disparagement of the community. At evening oblation, Ezra makes a public prayer. A crowd gathers around Ezra; and Shechaniah suggests the proposal of compelling a divorce. Ezra sanctions the proposal and a covenant is made to implement the proposal. At nightfall Ezra retreats to a temporary lodging place, one of the quarters in the temple cloisters, in which the temple officers lived.[63]

Days: 2 – 4 : 17th – 18th – 19th of the 9th Month

A proclamation was announced throughout Judah and Jerusalem to all the returned exiles that they should assemble at Jerusalem within three days (10:7-8).

Day 4: 20th of the 9th Month

It was the twentieth day of the nineth month when men of all Judah and Benjamin assembled at Jerusalem. The heavy rain (10:9) fell in the three winter months, Chislev, Tebet, Shebet, roughly December, January and February.[64] Batten suggested that it was Chislev, the early part of December.[65]

Day 14th : 1st day of the 10th Month

According to Batten, ten days lapsed before Ezra finalized his tribunal council, *i.e. 'the heads of the father's house'*. Thus, on the first day of the tenth month they sat down to investigate the matter.

Day ? : 1st day of the 1st Month

By the first day of the first month they had come to an end of all those that had married foreign women (10:17). The method of forced divorce had been successfully implemented (10:44).

Roughly estimated the narrative of the mixed marriage crisis and the implementation of forced divorce cover a period of three months and fourteen days.

Frequency of Events

Frequency specifies the number of times that an event in the story is recounted in the text. In considering the text of Ezra as being the work of an editor, *i.e.* the Chronicler, we find an elimination of repetitions. Many of the events are singulative, *i.e.* only repeated once. Even though there are similarities in the different rhetorical units, the response of the audience and the opposition, all have a singulative character.

Characterization

According to Rimmon-Kenan, characterization concerns the representation in the text of the character component of the story.[66] According to her theory, characterization can be described by assembling various character indicators distributed along the text-continuum, and when necessary inferring the traits from them. We have two basic character types presented through the text continuum of Ezra. Firstly, one which is presented through direct definition (*i.e.* by an adjective, abstract noun, part of speech etc.) and secondly, by an indirect presentation, through the character's action, speech, external appearance and habitual environment in which the character finds himself.

Characterization of Ezra

In this narrative analysis, we see Ezra as a *zealous* sustainer for the purity of Israel. We can understand the perceptions of Ezra since he is a Priest of Yahweh. From the text continuum, we note the two types of characterization analysis concerning Ezra. From a direct characterization (9:6), Ezra is ashamed to lift his face to God. Following the logic of the argument he is ashamed because of the state of the community. His shame overwhelms his ability to stand before God as a priest, the sustainer of the spiritual formation of Israel.

Through indirect characterization (- *i.e.* an evaluation of his actions), we perceive that Ezra is a *'radical puritist'*. To support this characterization we note in 9: 3-4 *'I rent my garments and mantle, pulled hair from my head and beard, and sat appalled'*, the radical perception of Ezra's character created by the author can be substantiated through his actions. The actions in *10:1 'confessing, weeping and casting himself'*, can justify his sympathetic characteristic towards the community. According to Batten, fasting in 10:6 *'neither eating bread, nor drinking water, for he was mourning'* was a common religious act by the priests.[67] Ezra's orientation reflects the priestly writer's obsession with 'separations' between the pure and the impure.[68]

In considering Ezra as a leader, the complexity of his skill as a prominent leader can be questioned. Throughout the major arguments in the narrative (especially in 10:8) Ezra is in the background, he was impelling the rulers to act. However, it is important to note that he sanctions the actions to divorce.

Characterization of the Offenders: The People of Israel

In analyzing the characteristics of the community of offenders we have a major shift in characteristics. In analyzing the direct presentation we note that in 9:2 'the holy race' and 9:8 'remnant', the offenders are seen in a positive characteristic evaluation. They are regarded as '*holy*' and '*remnant*' signifying the chosen people.

However, the characteristics of holiness stand in contrast to 9:14 'our evil deeds and for our great guilt'. The holy remnant is now regarded as *evil doers* and *transgressors against the law*. Their actions in 10:1 'people wept bitterly', 10:9 'trembling' and 10:13 'greatly transgressed' signify the acknowledgement of their current attributions.

Through an indirect analysis of the texts, we note in 9:4 'trembled at the words of the God of Israel' the trembling illuminates their guilt and fear.

The Foreign Wives

In analyzing the foreign wives we know that they are Canaanites, Hittites, Perizzites, Jebusites, Ammonites, Moabites, Egyptians and Amorites. From what we have gathered in the post-exilic times, it seems as though the surrounding people had taken advantage of the situation to encroach on Judean territory.

The author considers them as foreigners, thus giving them the characteristic of a stranger not known to Israel. Through direct characterization analysis, the author refers to them as 'the people of the land, with their abominations' (9:11). Clearly, we can see the characteristics of the foreign women - *i.e.* 'people of abominations' stand in contrast to the characteristics of the Judean men as being the 'holy race'.

In analyzing the indirect characterization, we note that in 9:12, the 'peace and prosperity' of these foreign women are mentioned. In considering these elements we can assume that the foreign women were highly influential on the Judean men due to their economic status. Thus, we can understand the need for the Judean men to be 'strong' (9:12) to overcome the attractive presentation of the foreign women. According to Williamson, the difficult economic circumstances that the returned exiles faced could soon have placed them at the mercy of these powerful foreigners.[69]

Focalization

Focalization is the angle of vision through which the story is filtered in the text, and is verbally formulated by the narrator.[70] Focalization in the text of Ezra 9-10 is distinguished from the narrator and narration. The reason being that even though a first (Ezra) or a third (Chronicler) person narrates the story, both use different characters in the represented world of the story as a focalizer character - *i.e. center of consciousness.*

Rimmon-Kenan noted in her analysis of focalization that narratives are not only focalized by someone but also on someone or something.[71] Example: In rhetorical unit 2, where Ezra is making a public prayer, the subject (focalizer) is Ezra, the agent whose perceptions orient the presentation, whereas the object (the focalized) is the transgression of the law (*i.e.* the marriage to foreign women), that which the focalizer perceives.

Rhetorical Unit 1:	*Focalizer*: Ezra
	Object :The state of the community
Rhetorical Unit 2:	*Focalizer*: Ezra
	Object: Transgression of the Law

Rhetorical Unit 3:	*Focalizer*: Shechaniah *Object*: Forced Divorce
Rhetorical Unit 4:	*Focalizer* : Ezra *Object*: Consequences of failing to attend the Assembly
Rhetorical Unit 5:	*Focalizer*: Offenders/Accused *Object*: Implementation of divorce
Rhetorical Unit 6:	*Focalizer* : Ezra *Object:* Selection of divorce tribunal
Rhetorical Unit 7:	Focalizer: Ezra *Object:* List of offenders.

Perceptual Facet

The perceptual facet is determined by time and space. In terms of time and space, the focalizers in Ezra 9-10 (namely: Ezra, Shechaniah and the offenders) are all internal and not external to the action and interaction. The focalizers do not provide a bird's-eye view of the action but participate in the action. From the list of focalizers above, in the relevant rhetorical units we note that these focalizers were active participants in the various arguments/discourses; therefore, they grant us a reflection of the actual situation.

The Psychological Facet

The psychological facet of perception has a cognitive and emotive component. The cognitive component (knowledge, conjecture, belief, memory) of the external narrator is that he knows everything about the represented world and about the mixed marriage crisis. However, the characters in the narrative are limited to this knowledge. They all function as internal focalizers with limited knowledge. This discrepancy creates a powerful effect on the reader, who shares the knowledge of the narrator in the Biblical narrative. The emotive component comprises the emotions of the internal focalizers. In Rhetorical unit 1, we note the emotions of Ezra - *i.e.* mourning, anger, remorse and shame, which is carried over to rhetorical unit 2. At the beginning of rhetorical unit 3, we note transference of emotions - *i.e.* weeping bitterly from Ezra to the audience that gathered around him.

This emotion of guilt is carried over to the assembly in rhetorical unit 6, where the congregation was trembling partly due to their guilt.

The Ideological Facet

The ideological facet of focalization comprises the norms of the text, which consist of a general system of viewing the world conceptually. Ideology defined in this context is a cultural formation or cultural production that expresses the point of view of a social class or caste.[72] In this narrative text of the mixed marriage crisis in the post-exilic Judean community, the narrator-focalizer's norms or ideology (*i.e.* the polemic against the foreign women) provide the single dominant perspective, which is taken as authoritative and all other ideologies within the text are evaluated from this higher position. In Ezra, the norms and ideology are all implicit in the orientation, which the narrator provides throughout the narrative, through implicit and explicit commentary as well as speech and actions of Ezra and the accused community.

The ideology of Ezra (foreign marriages as a transgression against the law) is positively evaluated by the narrator-focalizer and is the same as his own. The ideology is communicated to the narratee as the ideology, which the narratee must hold too. The focalization through the focalizers: Shechaniah and the accused community provide a similar ideological perspective, thus, the ideology for social transformation begins on the level of the 'grassroots' community.

Narrative Theory as Narration

Narration is the analytic category in narrative theory, which accounts for the act of narrating - *i.e.* telling the story. Following Rimmon-Kenan's development of the notions of the implied author and reader on the one hand, and the narrator and narratee on the other,[73] I accept her formulation of the notions of the narrator and the narrattee as relevant for my purpose. The narrator is the implicit addresser of the texts of Ezra, and the narratee is the implicit addressee. Minimally, the narrator can be defined as 'the agent, which at the very least narrates or engages in some activity serving the needs of the narration'.[74] The needs of the narration as they pertain to Ezra 9-10, are primarily determined by the narrator's perceptions of *time and space, the level of narration, the narrator's commentary, the narrator's cognition of objects and characters and the narrator's ideological norms and values.* In addition to these elements, the narration can be studied in terms of the nature of the speech representation in the narrative text.

In Ezra 9-10, narrative time is determined by 'ulterior narration'- *i.e.* the narrative events are narrated after they happened. The complaint laid, Ezra's prayer, the proposal, the summoning of the assembly, the assembly, the three month task and the list of offenders are narrated after they have occurred.

The level of narration in Ezra 9-10 is both extra-diegetic and diegetic. Using the source theory we can say that the whole narration of the mixed marriage crisis is extra-diegetic, due to the work of the Chronicler. However, in considering that Ezra's memoir was used, then it is also diegetic, since Ezra is an intra-diegetic character, who relates certain events (Ezra 9).

The narrator's commentary provides narrational explanations and commentary on the speech and action in the narrative. In 10:9 the trembling of the people is explained by the narrator's commentary. As such, it provides lines of direction and indirection to the reader or listener.

The narrator's cognition of objects and characters comprise the cognitive elements, which the narrator holds. The narrator's knowledge about the history of the remnant, the law, mix marriages and divorce are conveyed through the narrative to the narratee. The narrative structure and impact on the narratee is such that it wants to persuade the narratee to accept this knowledge too.

The narrator's ideological norms and values are also shared by the narratee. This is closely related to the previous point. These elements objectified and analyzed as part of the discourse of the narrator also form part of the interpretive community that the narrator represents. Such an objectification provides the interpreter with the contents of the post-exilic Judean community and their practices - *i.e.* divorce, used by the narrator and members of the Judean community.

In order to explain the speech representation in Ezra 9-10 we will use the theory of Rudolph that the book of Ezra was originally written by Ezra as a report to the Persian King. Therefore, the speech in Ezra is both diegetic and mimetic. In mimesis, the narrator creates the illusion that it is not he who speaks; he is only showing the actions (Ezra 10). However, in Chapter 9, the narrator does not create the illusion that it is not he who is speaking in his direct 'telling' of the story, his narration here is thus diegetic. In diegetic representation, the narrator does not hide the fact that he is the one who tells the story and that the views presented are his views.

A RHETORICAL CRITIQUE OF NEHEMIAH 13: 23-31

In the Nehemiah texts we come across a different situation. An internal struggle is not the issue with the Nehemiah material, the chief danger was perceived to come from the outside of Judah. Political considerations seem predominant in Nehemiah, giving the impression of treacherous power-struggle in both temple and government through strategic marriages. In Nehemiah, we are dealing with a specific case. Tobiah (the Ammonite) and Sanballat (the Horonite) were leaders of the opposition to Nehemiah's work of rebuilding Jerusalem. According to Williamson, the context clearly presupposes that they were the leaders of those already in the land and not part of the group who returned with Ezra. Therefore, he suggests that they were district governors.[75]

The question arises concerning the descent of Tobiah and Sanballat, which is crucial to the discussion. On onomastic grounds, it is supposed that Tobiah must be a Yahweh Worshipper.[76] However, according to Williamson's objection, Ammonite should be taken as an ethnic categorization.[77] In his analysis, he concludes that Sanballat was governor of Samaria, and is of Moabite origin, thus making both of them foreigners.

The example that Nehemiah chooses to illustrate the problems of foreign marriages is an example of political leadership - *i.e.* Solomon. From Nehemiah, we gain a strong impression that the problem of foreign marriages is centrally a political problem, involving Jewish aristocracy and local governmental leadership. According to Blenkinsopp, 'as sparse as our information is, it reveals a network of relationships cemented by '*marriages de convenance*' between the Sanballats, Tobiads, and important elements of the lay and clerical aristocracy in Jerusalem.[78]

What we are clearly dealing with in Nehemiah, is the attempt to inter-marry the leadership of the temple with the local political leadership, while in Ezra, we have no such suggestion. The example of Solomon is only cited in Nehemiah, which suggests an explicitly political concern in the Nehemiah texts. The politics of associating with the descendants of Ammon and Moab is also much more a reference to local leadership than is the case with Ezra, where the ethnic categories are more pejorative than informative.

Rudolph made a speculation on the socio-political goals that may have been sought through these alliances: 'community leaders, while aware of the negative implications of foreign wives, had no desire to sacrifice good relations with neighbours, or financial ties, for the sake of a principle'.[79] An examination of the Ezra-Nehemiah cases in relation to modern sociological studies of mixed marriages, has strongly suggested that the post-exilic community showed signs of disintegration and trauma, which was responded to by the attempts to *'shore up'* boundaries and remove economic and political temptations by pointing to their dire consequences in Israel's past.[80] The Nehemiah texts, however, raise a further possibility because of their specific attention to political and foreign leadership.

Rhetorical Unit/s

The larger rhetorical unit is Nehemiah 13, which deals wholly with reforms; effected by Nehemiah during his second administration. In this larger rhetorical unit, we have five smaller units: (a) the residence of Tobiah in the temple chamber, (b) the securing of tithes to the Levites so that they could give their services to the temple, (c) the prevention of traffic on the Sabbath, (d) the abolition of marriages to foreign women, and (e) the banishment of Sanballat's son-in-law.[81]

Within the larger rhetorical unit of Nehemiah 13, and his acts of administration, we have the mixed marriage crisis, which he encountered (13:23-31). This rhetorical unit is further divided into rhetorical unit (1a), the oath and covenant to stop the practices and rhetorical unit (1b), the banishment of Sanballat's son-in-law.

Rhetorical Unit 1: Mixed Marriage Crisis (Nehemiah 13:23-31)

In a composition of the larger rhetorical unit (13:23-31), Nehemiah discovers Judeans married to Philistine women (exogamous marriages) and their children were unable to speak the language of the people of Yahweh.

He punished the offenders severely and exacted an oath against the repetition of the offence. In this rhetorical unit, Nehemiah cites the case of Solomon's downfall linking to relationships with foreign women. The son-in-law of Sanballat, a grandson of Eliashib, was banished from Jerus. The rhetorical unit closes with general statements about temple ritual.

Rhetorical Unit 1a: Covenant and Oath not to Continue the Practices (Nehemiah 13:23 –27)

Language Disparagement (Nehemiah 13: 23-24)

The rhetorical unit opens with a social discourse to one of the terms recorded in the covenant, which was the decision not to take foreign women as their wives (10:30). It transcends with an encounter of Nehemiah discovering foreign marriages - *i.e.* Judean men married to women that were Ashodites, *Ammonites and Moabites. Ammonites and Moabites* seem to be a later edition of the Chronicler.[82]

These were people towards whom there was great political and social animosity (13:1). Therefore, these names were added by the Chronicler to climax the argument of this rhetorical unit. There may have been marriages with these ethnic groups, however, Ashodite in 13:24, shows that Nehemiah is dealing with a single class. Ashdod was one of the five Philistine cities that became incorporated into the Persian Empire. [83]

In consideration of Batten's analysis, these foreign relationships produced a corruption of speech - *i.e.* a *patois* – half-foreign and half Jewish.[84] According to Batten's analysis, the children spoke the language of their mothers.[85] The clause in Nehemiah 13:24 *'and they were not able to speak Jewish'* supports this view. Brockington argued that the importance of this situation being recorded as a social disparagement was due to the implication - *i.e.* foreign speech would alienate them from the Law and the synagogue.[86] A different aspect of the problem of mixed marriages is raised in this rhetorical unit: The importance of a language as an indication of the survival of the distinctive identity of a people (a modern conception to this theory of identity through language is Wales, whose defenders have felt it imperative to insist on the preservation of the language as a means of national identity).[87]

Nehemiah's Reaction and Covenant (Nehemiah 13:25)

The violence of the punishment shows how greatly Nehemiah was incensed: '*I cursed them and I smote certain of the...and I pulled out their hair*'. According to Isaiah 50:6, hair was pulled out usually from the beard, but in Ezra 9:3, both the hair from the head and the beard was pulled out as a sign of distress. The pulling out of hair according to Isaiah 50:6 would indicate that this was a regular form of punishment.[88] Coggins argued that the violent behaviour recorded in verse 25 should be regarded as largely ritual gestures of revulsion rather than an outbreak of emotion.[89] Apart from showing his anger in typical oriental fashion, all that Nehemiah felt able to do was to prevent recurrences of the practice in the future. This stands in contrast to Ezra's policy of divorce (Ezra 9-10). In contradiction to Ezra's actions, Nehemiah did not force the Judean men to divorce their wives to rectify the problem. He exacted an oath that they would stop these practices. As confusing as these actions may seem, one can justify the responses of Ezra and Nehemiah. Ezra was a priest and was concerned with the purity of Israel, which responded to other implications such as the land tenure system, which resulted in implications to the Judean Temple economy. Whereas, Nehemiah was a governor and concerned more with the identity crisis and the political implications of these mixed marriages.

In this rhetorical unit, we note that Nehemiah made the accused (*i.e.* those married to foreigners) take an oath to stop these practices. However, the Chronicler leaves us with no conclusion as to the result of this oath. What were the implications of this oath? Did it later result in a proposition of divorce to maintain the identity of the community?

An Allusion to Solomon (Nehemiah 13:26-27)

The example of Solomon is an allusion to 1 Kings 11, where his shortcomings are set out as a preliminary to an account of the division of the kingdoms of Israel and Judah. In the rhetorical unit, Solomon is quoted with political implications leading to the presentation of the argument in the following rhetorical unit. His relationships with foreign wives resulted in him going astray.[90] The placement of this allusion to Solomon seems to be added into the rhetorical argument to substantiate the political alliances of mixed marriages in Nehemiah's banishment of Sanballat's son-in-law.[91]

In considering that this allusion falls into rhetorical unit 1a, it is an addition of the Chronicler. Nehemiah is disturbed purely by the corruption of the language, and feared the Jewish people were in danger of loosing their identity.[92] In verse 27, we have the conclusion of Nehemiah's assumed address. Batten stated that as it stands the verse is barely translatable. He uses the vulgate translation, *'and shall we by disobedience* (referring to the record in the covenant 10:30) *do all this great evil that we should act insolently toward our God and marry foreign wives'.*[93]

Rhetorical Unit 1b: Banishment of Sanballat's Son-in-Law (Nehemiah 13:28-31)

We find in this rhetorical unit, a specific instance of a foreign alliance, which naturally aroused the governor. One of the sons of Joiada, the son of Eliashib the high priest, was a son-in-law of Sanballat the Horonite (13:28). The tension between Nehemiah and Eliashib is further illustrated. He had shown in verses 4-9, to be in league with one of Nehemiah's enemies, Tobiah, in this rhetorical unit he is shown related by marriage to Nehemiah's other contemporary namely, Sanballat.[94] The point illustrates the double problem faced by Nehemiah: (a) The urgency of maintaining purity, (b) the need for watchfulness against human enemies, who might find allies even within the holy community.

In the texts of Nehemiah (2:10, 3:33, 4:1, 6:1), Sanballat was one of the most troublesome of Nehemiah's enemies. It was by these alliances that developed with the foreign marriages that the enemy (Nehemiah's contemporaries: Sanballat and Tobiah) was kept posted with the activities of Nehemiah.[95]

The phrase *'I chased him from me'* implied that Nehemiah would not have him in his company, due to his refusal to co-operate. The name of the expelled priest is not given, but he may have been a brother of Jehohanan and named Jonathan (12:11, 23). Priests (and this one was in direct line of the high priesthood) had to be extra careful in marriage (a high priest could only marry a virgin of Israel). In this situation the grandson of Eliashib the high priest had performed an inofficious act by marrying a foreign woman (*i.e.* an act - *mix marriage*- not in accordance with moral duty). The crime of refusal to co-operate was worsened by the fact that Sanballat had shown himself an uncompromising political enemy of Nehemiah. Brockington argued that Nehemiah obviously felt confident of his standing with the king and of his duty both to God and to his fellow Jews, so to act against a fellow governor's son-in-law.[96] In verse 30: *'and I purified them from everything foreign'*, a reference to the priesthood regaining its integrity in the separation of men married to foreign women.[97] The ending of this rhetorical unit is abrupt, in the manner of many Old Testament books, but nevertheless positive, in the sense that the claim is made that despite all the obstacles put in the way, the work of restoration had been completed and its essentials maintained against all opposition.

Relational Posture of the Rhetorical Unit/s

In an analysis of the Nehemiah texts (13:23-31), we explore the relationships of modality and deixis to the network of intentions, which become a part of the background to the reading of Nehemiah's address of the mixed marriage crisis.

Modalities

In analyzing the conditions provided by the background, the norms, social values and desires and the communicant's believe and knowledge need to be taken into consideration. In Nehemiah 13:23-31 we find that the Chronicler uses the similar modals found in Ezra - *i.e.* cognitional and volitional modes.

Cognitional Modal

With respect to the cognitional modal the author and audience share:

An identity stasis: 'and they could not speak the language of Judah' 13:23.

Known traditions of the covenant: The oath taken to stop the practices of these *foreign relationships* (13:25) are a reinstatement of 10:30 that was listed in the covenant, where marriages to foreigners were prohibited.

A history of Israel: 'Did not Solomon king of Israel sin on such account' (13:26). Here we find a reference to the history of the political leadership of Israel. The author takes for granted that his audience understands the era he is relating too.

The polemic against foreign women: '...nevertheless foreign women made even him to sin' (13:26). From this clause we see that there is a polemic against the foreign women as being influential in deceiving the Judean men to conceive sin against Yahweh.

The integrity of the priesthood: In 13:29 the author states *'....because they have defiled the priesthood and the covenant of the priesthood'* thus implying that the integrity of the priesthood was compromised. The reinstating of this integrity is acknowledged after the expelling of the priest. We find the clause in 13:30: *'thus I cleansed them from everything foreign, and I established the duties of the priest...'*

Political alliances: The author assumes in 13:28 that his audience knows the status of the political alliance created by the grandson of the Eliashib, the high priest and Sanballat through the mix marriage (*cf* 2:10).

Volitional Modal

Within the volitional modal we see a directed discussion from Nehemiah within an atmosphere of condemnation. We find the following: authoritative command and shame (13:23-25), education and judgement (13:26), judgement and condemnation (13:28-30) and reward and retribution (13:29-31). In this rhetorical unit of Nehemiah we also find that the text is assertive upon its audience and the recipients (*i.e.* the audience) are passive, which stands in contrast to Ezra 10, where the audience is active in the discussion. Thus, in considering the relational posture (*i.e.* how does the text choose to relate itself to the audience?) we find the text affirmative, assertive and subordination oriented.

Deixis

In analyzing the orientation of the content of a sentence in relationship to time, place and personal participants the following *deixis* will be examined: (i) *personal deixis,* (ii) *intonational deixis,* (iii) *spatial deixis,* and (iv) *temporal deixis.*

Personal Deixis

The personal deixis is an examination of the author's use of person, demonstrative pronouns and personal names within the text.

Rhetorical Unit 1a: In 13:23, Nehemiah begins the rhetorical unit with *'I'* signifying a first hand account of his encounter with the mixed marriage crisis. He uses inclusive terminology to group those that have transgressed against the law and the covenant in 13:24 *'their'* and *'they'*, 13:25 *'them'*, *'their'*, *'yourselves'*. Later on, the righteous (*i.e.* those that kept the covenant), are set in distinction from the offenders: *'Shall we then listen to you'* (13:27).

Rhetorical Unit 1b: Although rhetorical unit 1b is a reference to an incident of one priest (singular) who was banished due to his foreign marriage, the author uses plural terminology.

13:29 – *'Remember them...because they...'*

13:30 – *'Thus I cleansed them...'*

According to Batten there was only one priestly offender mentioned, however, Nehemiah was not entirely concerned about the purity of the priesthood.[98] Jehoiada's son was not a grave offender because he was a priest, but because he had married Sanballat's daughter, the implications were political. According to the LXX Septuagint version, Nehemiah may have said: *'because they have sought kinship with the priesthood...'*[99] The imprecation would then be against the house of Sanballat and with possible recollection of Tobiah (13:4ff).

In this respect, one should also note the use of proper names and by referring to specific persons, types and places.

Proper Names:	Solomon (13:26) Jehoiada (13:28) Eliashib (13:28) Sanballat (13:28)
Social Groups:	Jews (13:23) Horonite (13:28) Priesthood (13:29) Levites (13:29)
Types:	King of Israel (13:25) Foreign Women (13:27) High Priest (13:28)
Places:	Ashdod, Ammon, Moab (13:23) Judah (13:24) Israel (13:26)

Intonational Deixis

The Author, Mixed Marriages and the Polemic against Foreign Women

In considering the evaluative attitude on the part of the author towards the given social polemic against the foreign women we find that the author clearly expresses his emotion and understanding of the mixed marriages as being evil. This we note in 13:27 -*'Great evil'*, *'act treacherously'*, which is set against defilement of the priesthood *'defiled the priesthood'* (13:29). The alliances created through these mixed marriages threatened the stability of the community as well as the purity and tradition of the priesthood. The marrying of a priest to a foreign woman placed the integrity of the priesthood in great danger. As the son of the high priest, would have been in direct genealogical lineage (through his father) of the priesthood.

Spatial Deixis

In spatial deixis we consider the geographical locations mentioned by Nehemiah. In 13:23 we have reference to the foreign women who were married to the Judean men being inhabitants from Ashdod, Ammon and Moab. These countries were also enemies of Israel. In Ezra 9-10, these women were part of the plot for the encroachment of Judean territory. The Jews were from Judah. A reference is also made to King Solomon of Israel (13:26).

Temporal Deixis

Nehemiah in 13: 26 highlights the future political status of Israel by referring to the past political history of Solomon and his marriages to foreign women. He questions the future in verse 27: *'shall we then listen to you and do all this great evil and act treacherously against our God by marrying foreign women?'* Nehemiah argues for the future manifestation of fulfilment in the life of the community as distinct from the consequences that emerged from Solomon's foreign marriages - *i.e.* foreign women causing Judean men to sin and act treacherously against the covenant. According to Nehemiah, due to the political alliance created by the marriage of Eliashib's grandson, it placed the integrity of the priesthood and the political status of the remnant in jeopardy. Mixed marriages should be set as a social boundary not to be crossed in order to sustain the establishment of the community.[100]

Method of Argumentation

In general we can assume that the intention of the author's argument centered on three aspects, namely (a) rhetorically assumed reality, (b) Quasi-logical argument, and (c) Real Politik.

Rhetorical Assumed Reality

Appealing to a historical structure of rhetorical reality, the author sets up his first argumentative position within the framework of Israel's dialect. In 13:23, the author uses the mixed marriage crisis to emphasize the language disparagement of that particular society. He sets the foundation for his argument based on the Judean dialect. The children of the mixed marriages could not speak the language of their fathers (13:24), as a result the reality assumed by the rhetoric is that the children would not be able to learn the laws or attend the synagogue. The author then uses this argument to establish a rhetorical reality, which is also based on the fact that the prohibition of mixed marriages was recorded in the covenant (10:30). The author then uses this assumed reality to substantiate his actions in 13:25 (*i.e.* the compelling of an oath to stop the practices of mixed marriages).

Quasi-logical Argument

Supported by the established rhetorical reality, the author introduces a digression based on Nehemiah's assessment of Solomon and his relationship with foreign women. The author uses a change of strategy. By introducing a quasi-logical argument to the past political state of Israel, which was influenced by King Solomon and his foreign marriages. He makes a contemporary application that foreign women influence Judean men to fall into sin. This argumentation with reference to a past incident builds upon his first argument and introduces the political implications to follow in his next argument.

Real Politik

In the latter rhetorical unit concerning the banishment of a priest, we find that Nehemiah's argument consists of politics based on reality and material needs, rather than on morals or ideals. The author establishes this argument by synchronizing the priest's marriage to a foreigner, and that he became a son-in-law to one of Nehemiah's political adversaries. In retrospect according to Batten, Nehemiah was not interested in the purity of the priesthood.[101] However, he uses the integrity of the priesthood, which was jeopardized by the priest's marriage to a foreigner to justify his actions of banishing the son-in-law of his political adversary. He combines a method of assumed rhetorical reality based on the fact that a high priest could only marry a virgin of Israel. In order to re-establish the purity of the priesthood he had to cleanse them from everything foreign (13:20).

The basic premise of his argument is highlighted in 13:29 *'remember them'* with reference to his political contemporaries.

Shifts in Argumentative Situation

In the first rhetorical unit (1a), Nehemiah encounters a mixed marriage crisis based on the social disparagement concerning language (13:13:23-24). He then shifts the argument to his analysis of Solomon's downfall linked to his marriages with foreign women (13:26). In 13:27, he shifts the argumentation to a response from the audience, which leads to the covenant and oath to stop the practices (13:25). Using the political discourse of Solomon he builds upon the banish-ment of a priest who had married the daughter of his political adversary, namely Sanballat (13:28). He uses this marriage alliance to argue the state of the priesthood, which has been defiled (13:29). He justifies his banishment with a shift to the re-establishment of the duties of the priests and Levites, thus re-establishing the priesthood. He then ends his argument based upon the principle of reward and retribution *'Remember me ...for good'* (13:31).

Classification of Argument

Narrative Analysis

Using the principle of narrative analysis established by Rimmon-Kenan, an analysis will be performed using the distinction between (a) story, (b) text, and (c) narration.

Narrative Theory as Story

In considering narrative theory as story, we will make a distinction between events in the story and characters in the story.

Events in the Story

In the story of the mixed marriage crisis encountered by Nehemiah in the course of his administration as governor, we have three events. The first event is Nehemiah's personal encounter with the children of the foreign relationships (13:23-24). The second event concerns Nehemiah's reaction and the compelling of people to take an oath to stop the practices of mixed marriages (13:25). The final event culminates with the banishment of a priest, the grandson of the high priest Eliashib, who married a Horonite woman - *i.e.* the daughter of Sanballat (13:28-31).

Characters in the Story

In this analysis we make a distinction between *flat* and *round* characters.

Characters	*Flat/Round*
Nehemiah	Round
Jews (Judean Men)	Flat
Foreign Women (Ashdod, Ammon & Moab)	Flat
King Solomon	Flat
Jehoiada	Flat
Eliashib	Flat
Banished Priest	Flat
Sanballat (the Horonite)	Flat

Narrative Theory as Text

In analyzing narrative theory as text, we make a distinction between (i) time, (ii) characterization, and (iii) focalization.

Time

In analyzing the time component of Nehemiah 13:23-31, we will focus on the following aspects, namely: *order, duration* and *frequency* of events.

Order of events: In order of events we find special reference to the analeptic (flashback) and proleptic (foreshadowing) relations between the story and text time. In Nehemiah 13:26, we find a flashback (analeptic reflection) to the monarchy of Solomon, this is with reference to 1 Kings 11. In the following verse 13:27, we find a foreshadowing of the future of the remnant. If they persist with the relationships to foreign women, then they will be acting treacherously against God and committing great evil.

Duration of events: In an analysis of duration, we consider the length of time an event takes in the story and textual levels. In reading the narrative of Nehemiah's mixed marriage crisis we find that the textual level is longer than the story level. On the story level it seems as though time is inescapably linear. However, these actions listed in Nehemiah 13 are reforms that took place under his administration. The banishment of the grandson Eliashib would have taken much longer than the time it takes the reader to read about it. In considering the political tension that has built up between Sanballat and Nehemiah, the expulsion of Sanballat's son-in-law would be a result of the culmination over a period of animosity created between the two governors that surfaced in various circumstances and situations of their administration. Also, the re-establishment of the priesthood was probably a long process. However, to the reader it would seem as though it was a short-term assessment.

Frequency of events: In Nehemiah 13:23-31, we find that the events are singulative. There are no similarities between the rhetorical units. The repetition of events may have been eliminated by the work of the Chronicler/Editor.

Characterization

In Nehemiah 13:23-31, the characterization of the *round* and *flat* characters takes place primarily through their actions, speech and analogy in the names or labels applied to them.

Firstly, in analyzing the character of Nehemiah, we note that through his actions - *i.e.* '*And I contended with them and cursed them and beat some of them and pulled out their hair, and made the...*' (13:25), that Nehemiah was an aggressive governor. He made them take an oath. It was not a voluntary action. He compelled the oath upon them similar to Ezra mandating a divorce. However, his actions of compelling an oath and banishing a priest are regarded as good actions in 13:31 '*Remember me...for good*' which would justify that Nehemiah according to his reformations was a good governor. Nehemiah stands in contrast to the characteristics of Ezra. Ezra stood behind his leaders compelling them to take action. However,

Nehemiah displays greater leadership characteristics. He stood at the forefront of his actions. He disciplined and reprimanded the guilty and *'chased'* the priest. We find a contrast to the leadership skills of Ezra. Nehemiah is assertive.

However, Ezra is more of a pragmatist than Nehemiah. Nehemiah was confronted with a situation of mixed marriages. He sought the rectification of the problem through the compelling of an oath. The question arises whether this was a successful pragmatic application. Ezra on the other hand was a pragmatist. He saw a problem and sought a solution that was implemented to counteract the problem.

In 13:26, Solomon king of Israel is used as an example of a righteous person *i.e. '...no king like him...beloved by his God'*, stands in contrast to his sinful nature after he had married foreign women. Although, there is no direct characterization of the foreign women, the acts of marrying them are characterized as *'great evil'* and *'treacherous'* (13:27). Through this indirect characterization and with reference to 13:26 *'foreign women made even him to sin'*, the foreign women are seen as deceivers of the Judean men. The priest who had married the daughter of Sanballat (foreign woman) was seen as a defiler of the priesthood - *i.e.* 13: 29 *'Remember them ...because they have defiled the priesthood...'*

Focalization

In considering that focalization is the angle of vision through which the story is filtered in the text, and is verbally formulated by the narrator, focalization in the text of Nehemiah 13: 23-31 is distinguished from the narrator and narration. The reason being that even though a first or a third narrates the story both use different characters in the represented world of the story as a focalizer character - *i.e. center of consciousness.*

Narratives are not only focalized by someone but also on someone or something.[102] In rhetorical unit 1(a), the focalizer is Nehemiah and the object is the language disparagement with specific reference to the children of the foreign marriages. In rhetorical unit 1(b) the focalizer is Nehemiah, however, the object is the defilement of the priesthood and the intermarriage of the temple with a political adversary.

Perceptual Facet

The perceptual facet is determined by time and space. The focalizer in Nehemiah is internal and not external to the action and interaction. The focalizer does not provide a bird's-eye view of the action but participates in the action.

The Psychological Facet

In considering that the Nehemiah texts are the work of the Chronicler/ editor we find that the psychological facet of perception has a cognitive and emotive component. The cognitive component of the external narrator is that he knows everything about the represented world and about the mixed marriage crisis in both Ezra and Nehemiah. However, the characters in the narrative are limited to this knowledge. They all function as internal focalizers with limited knowledge.

The emotive component comprises the emotions of the internal focalizer. In Rhetorical unit 1(a), we note the emotions of Nehemiah, *i.e.* anger, remorse, shame and frustration (13:23-24).

The Ideological Facet

In this narrative text of the mixed marriage crisis in the post-exilic Judean community, the narrator-focalizer's norms or ideology provide a dominant perspective, which is taken as authoritative. In Nehemiah, the norms and ideology are all implicit in the orientation.

The ideology of Nehemiah (foreign marriages as a transgression against the law and the covenant) is positively evaluated by the narrator-focalizer and is the same as his own. The ideology is communicated to the narratee as the ideology, which the narratee must hold too. Evident in Nehemiah is the threat that mixed marriages posed to the stability of the Judean community as a whole. Thus, this culminated in an ideology of the polemic against foreign women and foreign marriages that threatened the stability of the community and the priesthood.

Narrative Theory as Narration

The needs of the narration as they pertain to Nehemiah 13:23-31, are primarily determined by the narrator's perceptions of *time and space, the level of narration, the narrator's cognition of objects and characters and the narrator's ideological norms and values and the nature of speech representation.*

In Nehemiah 13: 23-31, narrative time is determined by 'ulterior narration' - *i.e.* the narrative events are narrated after they happened. Nehemiah's encounter with the language disparagement, the covenant and oath to stop the practices and the banishing of the priest are narrated after they have occurred.

The level of narration in Nehemiah 13 is both extra-diegetic and diegetic. Using the source theory we can say that the whole narration of the mixed marriage crisis is extra-diegetic, due to the work of the Chronicler. However, in considering that Nehemiah's memoir was used as a source, then it is also diegetic, since Nehemiah is an intra-diegetic character; who relates all the events.

The narrator's cognition of objects and characters comprises the cognitive elements, which the narrator holds. The narrator's knowledge about the history of the law, the covenant and history of Solomon's reign as king of Israel is conveyed through the narrative to the narratee. The narrative structure and impact on the narratee is such that it wants to persuade the narratee to accept this knowledge.

The narrator's ideological norms and values are also shared by the narratee. This is closely related to the previous point. These elements objectified and analyzed as part of the discourse of the narrator also form part of the interpretive community that the narrator represents. Such an objectification provides the interpreter with the contents of the post-exilic Judean community, the integrity of the priesthood and the political status the community with regards to its political adversaries.

In order to explain the speech representation in Nehemiah we will use the theory that the book of Nehemiah was originally written by Nehemiah as a report to the Persian King of his activities during his administration as governor. Therefore, the speech in Nehemiah is diegetic. In diegetic representation, the narrator does not hide the fact that he is the one who tells the story and that the views presented are his views.

CONTEXTUAL MEANING : HISTORICAL RECONSTRUCTION OF EZRA 9-10 & NEHEMIAH 13

Perspectives on Ezra 9-10 & Nehemiah 13 from Modern Israel

By 'historical reconstruction' I refer to one of the many possible contextual situations in which the texts might be read and an analysis compared. To examine the subject further we turn to contemporary analogues for the situation in Judah during the fifth century BCE. According to Eisenstadt, social patterns and meanings in a particular culture will often persist under differing guises and continue to demarcate that society from other groups.[103] With this in mind, we can examine the developments in another Jewish society, which, like the post-exilic community had undertaken to return to the land. Developments in the twentieth century Israel provide a singularly vital data base as well as a useful sociological model for an analysis and undertaking of Ezra and Nehemiah.

According to Eisenstadt, patterns characteristic of the Jewish society took shape during the Second Temple period.[104] Therefore examining modern Israel is uniquely useful for understanding post-exilic phenomena. Also, twentieth century Israel relives some of the conditions, developments and events that had led to the formation of post-exilic Judah. Both communities are the products of re-surgence, of immigration in response to new possibilities for self-determination. In the earlier part of the twentieth century, the British Empire replaced the Ottomans as rulers of the Middle East, mirroring the takeover of the Persians in the sixth century BCE. As Judah was a strategic doorway for Persia in its dealings with Egypt and Greece, so this land became an important gateway for the British.[105]

The Balfour Declaration in 1917, in which the British Government promised the Jews a Jewish homeland, compares with Cyrus' edict, authorizing the Jews to return to Judah (Ezra 1). In both instances, immigration to Israel followed. New opportunities stimulated Jews from Christian Europe to return to Israel in large numbers. As a result of new arrivals, tension developed in the land between Jews and non-Jews. In this new mixture of population, three different intermarriage patterns were discovered.[106] Each provides a possible analogue to the controversy over the 'foreign wives' in Ezra 9-10 and Nehemiah 13:23-31.

Firstly, tension between Jews from different ethnic back-grounds. These dynamics suggest parallels to ethnic/cultural tension in the Persian period between Jews who had been exiled and those who stayed in the land, irrespective of specific religious practices. Secondly, tensions between Jews and non-Jews. Some opponents of the Jewish immigrants have been long-time settlers in the land and consider themselves native. These groups have their counterpart in the Persian period Judah. All of them have been involved in inter-marriages that have incurred formal and informal opposition. Thirdly, tension between orthodox and non-orthodox Jews on account of different religious perspectives. The basic conflict among these groups pertains to issues of authority and interpretation of the Torah, paralleling different religious practices and interpretations in the Persian period.

Although all three sets of the tension need to be investigated in order to discern the fuller complexity of the post-exilic situation, this historical reconstruction will focus only on the third. It will examine modern inner Jewish tension and in particular the modern phenomena of the *Haredim* as an analogue to Ezra 9-10. The term *'haredim'* literally means *'those who tremble'*. The word occurs in Ezra 10:3, where it refers to the pious supporters of Ezra. In modern Israel the term designates an ultra-orthodox Jewish movement. The movement is noted for their separate lifestyle coupled with an aggressive programme to impose their interpretation of Judaism upon other segments of the society, a situation that has led to intense inner Jewish conflict in Israel.[107]

According to Liebman, in March, 1988, 58 per cent of a random sample of Jews in Jerusalem identified religious-secular relations as the most serious problem in the city. The rise of the *Haredim* in Israel presents suggestive parallels to Ezra and Nehemiah. The emergence of this movement in modern Israel goes back to the time when Israel, as Palestine, first became part of the British Empire. Although the British Mandate, from a Jewish perspective, cannot be equated with the purportedly benign Persian rule, several interesting parallels exist.[108]

Gottwald suggests the parallel, when he refers to Israel as in the Persian era as *'Colonial Israel'*.[109] Like post-exilic Judah, the modern land of Israel that the British acquired contained diverse ethnic, religious and political groups. For both Empires, the strip of land served as a gateway to an important part of the Empire (*i.e.* to India for the British and to Egypt and Greece for Persia). In both instances, tensions between earlier settlers established on the land and Jewish newcomers flared up and required Imperial intervention.[110]

In this historical reconstruction, we limit the research to tracing the relation between what sociological studies call *'secularist'* and *'orthodox Jews'*.[111] Orthodoxy in Israel first gained official power when the British pressure led to the formation of the Chief Rabbinate as the highest religious authority for the Jewish sector. The British government saw the Jewish settlement, above all, as a religious community.[112] With the British patronage, the Chief Rabbinate fought against other Jewish groups for complete control over marriage and divorce laws.

In the mid 1930s, immigration from Poland and Lithuania brought to Israel great orthodox rabbis whose religious authority was not official or governmental but rather based upon spontaneous recognition by certain religious communities.[113] The greatest among them refused official position within the Chief Rabbinate. However, within a short time, they and not the official structures came to exert great religious power and authority in Israel. Practices within many religious communities depended on the decisions of the Eastern European orthodox rabbis rather than those of the official Chief Rabbinate. Over a period of time, the name *Haredim* (Ezra 9:4 and 10:3) came to designate these groups.[114]

In the meantime, the sphere of control by the Chief Rabbinate grew beyond its initial limits. By 1948, every Jewish citizen of the newly founded Israel had to marry in accordance with the laws determined by the Chief Rabbinate.[115] This represented a shift from the earlier vagueness in the legal structure under which one could bypass rabbinical authority. Prior to the establishment of the state, the definition of who was under the jurisdiction of the Chief Rabbinate was still flexible.

For the purpose of regulating family laws and for the sake of the *'Law of the Return'*, it eventually was deemed necessary to determine more definitely who is a Jew. A struggle led to a specific legal definition in 1970, and ironically to intensification of the problems. According to Segre, the government was confronted with two problems.[116] Firstly, they were confronted with the problem of the definition of a Jew with reference to the *Law of Return*, which grants immediate citizenship, to any Jew returning to his ancestral land. Secondly, concerns the definition of the Jew with reference to the competence of the religious courts in matters of marriage and divorce.

On March 10, 1970, the state of Israel, ruled that it would recognize as a Jew, only a person who has been born to a Jewish mother or who has been converted to Judaism and is not a member of another religion.[117] Prior to 1970, self-definition allowed persons to declare themselves Jews and be registered as such. However, the Chief Rabbinate could reject the legitimacy of such identity, when it came to the question of marriages, as only a Jew could marry a Jew.

After 1970, people who had considered themselves as Jews and had been legally considered as Jews by the state, found themselves legally outside the community of Israel, and unable to marry other Jews. The Chief Rabbinate could accept or reject candidates for marriage on the basis of its interpretation of the law as to who is a Jew. Since the authority of the Chief Rabbinate on questions of marriage is higher than that of the Supreme Court, it has voided marriages even after the Supreme Court had sanctioned them.

Nevertheless, the Chief Rabbinate, which is orthodox, on occasion appeared too moderate for the *Haredim*. Its authority declined and its rulings were superceded by the *Haredim*; by the teachings of the European rabbis and their disciples. The *Haredim* have called non-orthodox Jews 'gentiles' and denied their Jewish identity. From a *Haredi* perspective, a marriage between a *Haredi* and a *non-Haredi* constitutes a mixed marriage.[118] Although for the purpose of comparison, we have greatly simplified the complexities of the modern situation, three aspects of that situation are significant for our present situation. Firstly, the evolving definition of who is a Jew, moving from a broad category to a narrow one; secondly, the inter-religious gap that leads one group of Jews to characterize the other formally and publicly as gentiles and strangers; and thirdly, the dynamics and particular pace of such developments.

In the 1990s, almost 45 years after the establishment of the state of Israel, 55 years since the arrival of the ultra-orthodox Eastern European rabbis, and 74 years after the Balfour Declaration, the Jewish community in Israel is divided into at least four important groups - *i.e. Haredim, Orthodox, Religious Liberals and Non-Religious.*[119]

The phenomenon of the modern *Haredim* illustrates striking parallels to Ezra. As the British established the Chief Rabbinate for Jewish affairs, so we can suppose, the Persians created a structure for the Jewish affairs - *i.e. the priesthood.* Like the illustrious *haredi* European rabbis in the 1930s, Ezra arrived from the Diaspora late, after certain patterns had been established. He offered a more stringent definition of who is a Jew, which gained popular support among some segments of the population, leading to further legal reformation of the issues and to communal tension. In this process, previously sanctioned relationships had to be re-evaluated.

Using this example of the *Haredim* as an historical reconstruction, we also delineate a process - gradual and often tragic - by which some women, caught in the drama of shifting concepts of identity, can be transformed from spouses to strangers.

CONCLUSION

In considering the ethics of the forced divorce, Batten has pointed out the evil consequences of mixed marriages, in that they tended to threaten the imperfectly established solidarity of the community and the development of the religious life.[120] As a result Ezra compelling a divorce and Nehemiah exacting an oath should be analyzed as a *eudemonistic* approach (*i.e.* a system of ethics basing moral obligation on likelihood that actions will produce happiness). But actions cannot be judged from a consideration of their consequences (*i.e.* foreign women as a threat to the stability of the Judean temple economy or the political alliances created through these marriages).

In the analysis of Ezra and Nehemiah, we discover that emerging in the concepts of forced divorce and the polemic against the foreign women is an ideology. A false consciousness or an obfuscated mental process in which men (Ezra, Nehemiah and the Chronicler), do not understand the forces that actually guide their thinking, but imagine it to be wholly governed by logical and intellectual influences. When, thus deluded, the thinker is unaware that all thought, and particularly his own, is subject in its course and outcome to extra-intellectual social conditions, which it expresses in a form distorted by the interests and preferences of some collectivity or other.[121]

A large number of unmarried men may have come back from the

exile, and the provision of wives for them may have been a serious problem. In spite of the classic story of Solomon's downfall (Nehemiah 13:26), the position of a Jewish wife was not such as to make her an influential factor in the religious life of the nation. Initially in the narrative, it seems as though there was a large number of offenders. However, there are only 111 names in the list (Ezra 10:18-44), an inconsiderable number for the whole Judean province.[122]

One may well doubt, though, whether any good resulted from such a drastic course - *i.e.* forced divorce, and rejoice in the development of more humane methods of dealing with social problems, even if these reforms came slowly. In these texts we find that divorce was a socially acceptable institution. However, we find a contrary system of ethics towards divorce in the New Testament, especially in the confrontation between Jesus and the Pharisees. According to Childs, *'there are times in which the historical and literary questions can be left unresolved without jeopardizing the hearing of the Biblical message'*.[123]

NOTES

1. Watson D & Hauser A, *Rhetorical Criticism of the Bible*, EJ Brill, New York, 1994, p.62.
2. Culler J, *Literary Theory*, Oxford University Press, New York, 1997, p.83.
3. Ibid. pp.84-86.
4. Ibid. p.85.
5. Brockington LH, *Ezra, Nehemiah and Ester*, Thomas Nelson and Sons, England, 1969, p.106.
6. Eskenazi TC & Richards KH, *Second Temple Studies: 2 Temples and Community in the Persian period*, JSOT Press, Sheffield, England, 1994, pp.220-221.
7. Brockington LH, *Ezra, Nehemiah and Ester*, Thomas Nelson and Sons, England, 1969, p.105.
8. Ibid. p.106.
9. Ibid. p.107.
10. Ibid. p.107.
11. Ibid. p.108.
12. Batten LW, *A Critical Exegetical Commentary on the Books of Ezra and Nehemiah*, T&T Clark, Edinburg, 1961, p.335.
13. Ibid. p.336.
14. Ibid. pp.336-337.
15. Coggins RJ, *The Books of Ezra and Nehemiah*, Cambridge University Press, Cambridge, 1976, pp. 58-59.

16. Batten LW, *A Critical Exegetical Commentary on the Books of Ezra and Nehemiah*, T&T Clark, Edinburg, 1961, p.336.
17. Ibid. p.336.
18. Ibid. p.340.
19. Coggins RJ, *The Books of Ezra and Nehemiah*, Cambridge University Press, Cambridge, 1976, pp. 62-63.
20. Brockington LH, *Ezra, Nehemiah and Ester*, Thomas Nelson and Sons, England, 1969, p.110.
21. Ibid. p.110.
22. Batten LW, *A Critical Exegetical Commentary on the Books of Ezra and Nehemiah*, T&T Clark, Edinburg, 1961, p.340.
23. Ibid. p.340.
24. Brockington LH, *Ezra, Nehemiah and Ester*, Thomas Nelson and Sons, England, 1969, p.111.
25. Ibid. p.111.
26. Batten LW, *A Critical Exegetical Commentary on the Books of Ezra and Nehemiah*, T&T Clark, Edinburgh, 1961, p.341.
27. Ibid. p.342.
28. Ibid. p.342.
29. Ibid. p.343.
30. Ibid. p.344.
31. Ibid. p.344.
32. Ibid. p.345.
33. Ibid. p.346.
34. Brockington LH, *Ezra, Nehemiah and Ester*, Thomas Nelson and Sons, England, 1969, p.113.
35. Ibid. p.113.
36. Ibid. p.113.
37. Batten LW, *A Critical Exegetical Commentary on the Books of Ezra and Nehemiah*, T&T Clark, Edinburg, 1961, p.347.
38. Douglas M, *In the Wilderness: The doctrine of Defilement in the Book of Numbers, Journal for the Study of Old Testament*, (Supplement series 158), Sheffield Academic Press, Sheffield, 1993.
39. Brockington LH, *Ezra, Nehemiah and Ester*, Thomas Nelson and Sons, England, 1969, p.114.
40. Refers to a modal or method of procedure.
41. Perelman C, Olbrechts-Tyteca L, *The New Rhetoric: A Treatise on Argumentation*, University of Notre Dame Press, Notre Dame, 1971, p.154.
42. Wuellner W, *Reading Romans in Context*, Unpublished essay distributed to the SNTS Semina on Reader Response Criticism, 1987, pp.13-19.
43. Refers to an action or faculty of knowing, perceiving or conceiving.
44. Refers to an exercise of the will or power of the willing.
45. Batten LW, *A Critical Exegetical Commentary on the Books of Ezra and Nehemiah*, T&T Clark, Edinburg, 1961, p.336.
46. Wuellner W, *Reading Romans in context*, unpublished essay distributed to the SNTS Semina on Reader Response Criticism, 1987, p.14.
47. Brockington LH, *Ezra, Nehemiah and Ester*, Thomas Nelson and Sons, England, 1969, p.107.

48. Hester J, *Re-discovering and Re-inventing Rhetoric*, Scriptura, Journal of Bible and Theology in Southern Africa, Vol. 50, (July) 1994, p.12.
49. *Cf.* p. 86 of Chapter 3.
50. Christopher S, *The Mixed Marriage Crisis in Ezra*, in Eskenazi TC & Richards KH, *Second Temples Studies: 2 Temple and Community in the Persian period*, JSOT Press, Sheffield, England, 1994, p.256.
51. Batten LW, *A Critical Exegetical Commentary on the Books of Ezra and Nehemiah*, T&T Clark, Edinburg, 1961, p.344.
52. Wuellner W, *Reading Romans in context*, unpublished essay distributed to the SNTS Semina on Reader Response Criticism, 1987, p.15.
53. Christopher S, *The Mixed Marriage Crisis in Ezra*, in Eskenazi TC & Richards KH, *Second Temple Studies: 2 Temples and Community in the Persian period*, JSOT Press, Sheffield, England, 1994, p.244.
54. Ibid. p.244.
55. Brockington LH, *Ezra, Nehemiah and Ester*, Thomas Nelson and Sons, England, 1969, p.113.
56. Alter R, *The Art of Biblical Narrative*, George Allen and Unwin, London, 981.
57. Rimmon-Kenan S, *The Art of Biblical Narrative*, George Allen and Unwin, Methuen, London, 1983.
58. Ibid. p.40ff.
59. Ibid. p.41.
60. Ibid. p.43.
61. Genette G, *Narrative Discourse*, Blackwell, Oxford, 1972, p.33.
62. Batten LW, *A Critical Exegetical Commentary on the Books of Ezra and Nehemiah*, T&T Clark, Edinburg, 1961, pp.330-331.
63. Ibid. p.341.
64. Brockington LH, *Ezra, Nehemiah and Ester*, Thomas Nelson and Sons, England, 1969, p.112.
65. Batten LW, *A Critical Exegetical Commentary on the Books of Ezra and Nehemiah*, T&T Clark, Edinburg, 1961, p.343.
66. Rimmon-Kenan S, *The Art of Biblical Narrative*, George Allen and Unwin, Methuen, London, 1983, p.43.
67. Batten LW, *A Critical Exegetical Commentary on the Books of Ezra and Nehemiah*, T&T Clark, Edinburg, 1961, p.341.
68. Smith DL, *Religion and the Landless*, Meyer-Stone, Bloomington, 1989, pp.145-149.
69. Williamson HGM, *Ezra and Nehemiah*, Sheffield Academic Press, England, 1987, p.160.
70. Rimmon-Kenan S, *The Art of Biblical Narrative*, George Allen and Unwin, Methuen, London, 1983, p.43.
71. Ibid. p.74.
72. Clines DJA, *Interested Parties: The ideology of Writers and Readers of the Hebrew Bible*, *Journal for the study of Old Testament*, Supplement Series 205, Gender, Culture, Theory 1, Sheffield Academic Press, England, 1995.
73. Ibid. p.86.
74. Ibid. p.88ff.
75. Williamson HGM, *Ezra, Nehemiah*, Waco, Texas, 1985, p.130.

76. See Ackroyd's comments in 'Tobiah', *Harper's Bible Dictionary*, Harper & Row, New York, 1985, p.1080.
77. Williamson HGM, *Ezra, Nehemiah*, Waco, Texas, 1985, pp.182-183.
78. Blenkinsopp J, *Ezra-Nehemiah*, SCM Press, London, 1988.
79. Rudolph W, *Esra-Nehemia*, P. Siebeck, HAT, Tübingen, 1949, p.160.
80. Ezkenazi TC & Judd PE, *Marriage to a Stranger in Ezra 9-10*, in Eskenazi TC & Richards KH, *Second Temple Studies: 2 Temples and Community in the Persian period*, JSOT Press, Sheffield, England, 1994, p.261.
81. Batten LW, *A Critical Exegetical Commentary on the Books of Ezra and Nehemiah*, T&T Clark, Edinburg, 1961, p.286.
82. Ibid. p.299.
83. Brockington LH, *Ezra, Nehemiah and Ester*, Thomas Nelson and Sons, England, 1969, p.211.
84. Batten LW, *A Critical Exegetical Commentary on the Books of Ezra and Nehemiah*, T&T Clark, Edinburg, 1961, p.299.
85. Ibid. p.299.
86. Brockington LH, *Ezra, Nehemiah and Ester*, Thomas Nelson and Sons, England, 1969, p.211.
87. Coggins RJ, *The Books of Ezra and Nehemiah*, Cambridge University Press, Cambridge, 1976, p.143.
88. Batten LW, *A Critical Exegetical Commentary on the Books of Ezra and Nehemiah*, T&T Clark, Edinburg, 1961, p.300.
89. Coggins RJ, *The Books of Ezra and Nehemiah*, Cambridge University Press, Cambridge, 1976, p.143.
90. Batten LW, *A Critical Exegetical Commentary on the Books of Ezra and Nehemiah*, T&T Clark, Edinburg, 1961, p.301.
91. Ibid. p.301.
92. Ibid. p.301.
93. Ibid. p.301.
94. Coggins RJ, *The Books of Ezra and Nehemiah*, Cambridge University Press, Cambridge, 1976, p.144.
95. Ibid. p.143.
96. Brockington LH, *Ezra, Nehemiah and Ester*, Thomas Nelson and Sons, England, 1969, p.212.
97. Ibid. p.112.
98. Batten LW, *A Critical Exegetical Commentary on the Books of Ezra and Nehemiah*, T&T Clark, Edinburg, 1961, p.302.
99. Ibid. p.301.
100. Christopher S, *The Mixed Marriage Crisis in Ezra*, in Eskenazi TC & Richards KH, *Second Temples Studies: 2 Temple and Community in the Persian period*, JSOT Press, Sheffield, England, 1994, p. 244.
101. Batten LW, *A Critical Exegetical Commentary on the Books of Ezra and Nehemiah*, T&T Clark, Edinburg, 1961, p.302.
102. Ibid. p.74.
103. Eisenstadt SN, *Comments on the problem of continuity of Jewish historical patterns in Israeli society*, in Kahane R and Kopstein S (eds), *Problems of collective identity and legitimation in the Israeli society: A Reader*, Academon, Jerusalem, 1980, pp.381-396.

104. Ibid. p.389.
105. Ezkenazi TC & Judd PE, *Marriage to a Stranger in Ezra 9-10*, in Eskenazi TC & Richards KH, *Second Temples Studies: 2 Temples and Community in the Persian period*, JSOT Press, Sheffield, England, 1994, p.277.
106. Ibid. p.278.
107. Ibid. p.279.
108. Ibid. p.280.
109. Gottwald NK, *The Hebrew Bible: A Socio-Literary introduction*, Fortress Press, Philadelphia, 1985, pp. 409-590.
110. Ezkenazi TC & Judd PE, *Marriage to a Stranger in Ezra 9-10*, in Eskenazi TC & Richards KH, *Second Temples Studies: 2 Temples and Community in the Persian period*, JSOT Press, Sheffield, England, 1994, p.280.
111. Smith M, *Palestine Parties and Politics that shaped the Old Testament*, Columbia University Press, New York, 1971.
112. Ezkenazi TC & Judd PE, *Marriage to a Stranger in Ezra 9-10*, in Eskenazi TC & Richards KH, *Second Temples Studies: 2 Temples and Community in the Persian period*, JSOT Press, Sheffield, England, 1994, p.281.
113. Ibid. p.281.
114. Ibid. p.281.
115. Friedman M, *The Chief Rabbinate-Dilemma without solution*, in Kahane R and Kopstein S (eds), *Problems of collective identity and legitimation in the Israeli society: A Reader*, Academon, Jerusalem, 1980, pp.253-267.
116. Segre DV, *A Crisis of identity: Israel and Zionism*, Oxford University Press, Oxford, 1980, p.124.
117. Ezkenazi TC & Judd PE, *Marriage to a Stranger in Ezra 9-10*, in Eskenazi TC & Richards KH, *Second Temple Studies: 2 Temples and Community in the Persian period*, JSOT Press, Sheffield, England, 1994, p.284.
118. Weller L, Weller TS, *Strange Bedfellows: A Study of Mixed Religious Marriages*, in Liebman CS (ed), *Religious and Secular: Conflict and Accommodation between Jews in Israel*, Keter, Jerusalem, 1990, p.11.
119. Ezkenazi TC & Judd PE, *Marriage to a Stranger in Ezra 9-10*, in Eskenazi TC & Richards KH, *Second Temple Studies: 2 Temples and Community in the Persian period*, JSOT Press, Sheffield, England, 1994, pp.284-285.
120. Batten LW, *A Critical Exegetical Commentary on the Books of Ezra and Nehemiah*, T&T Clark, Edinburg, 1961, p.351.
121. Barr J, *History and Ideology in the Old Testament: Biblical Studies at the end of a Millennium*, Oxford University Press, Oxford, 2000.
122. Ibid. p.351.
123. Childs BS, *Introduction to Old Testament as Scripture*, SCM Press, London 1979, p.637.

4

KINGDOM ETHICS *VS* SECULAR ETHICS—RHETORICAL CRITICISM OF NEW TESTAMENT TEXTS

INTRODUCTION

The objective of this introduction is to sketch out the dimensions involved in studying the Gospels (Matthew/Mark/Luke) for the purpose of gaining some understanding of the institutions of marriage and divorce that prevailed in the time of the New Testament. The meaning of the words used in the Gospels, is derived from the general social system of the speakers of the language.[1] This results in what one says and what one means to say can often be quite different, especially for persons not sharing the same social system.

Trying to understand the writings of the Gospels, in a mature scholarly way is much like trying to understand a group of foreigners somewhere dropped in our midst. Nearly all scholarly aids to understanding the Bible offer information about who, what, when, where and how regarding these foreign writings. Such information is valuable and highly necessary.

In the context of this research, we find in Luke 16:18, a reference to the institutions of divorce and marriage that prevailed in that particular society. An analysis of these institutions forms the background to the discourse between Jesus and the Pharisees in Matthew 19:1-12 and Mark 10:1-12. According to Malina, New Testament writings can generate understanding only if we pay careful attention to the cultural systems that created them and which they embody.[2] In recent years, we have come to understand more clearly that the situation in which an utterance is produced is of great significance, and the words used are to some extent to be 'explained' by the 'context' in which they are designed to be or have actually been spoken in a linguistic interchange.[3]

In order to understand the dialogue between Jesus and the Pharisees it is imperative that we examine the understanding of divorce amongst the Jewish people present in that particular society. Hence, before I attempt an application of the rhetorical critical exegesis, I will provide an anthropological insight into the understanding of divorce and marriage in the world of the Gospels and an analysis of the literary context of the Gospels.

INSIGHTS OF THE NEW TESTAMENT WORLD FROM A CULTURAL ANTHRO-POLOGICAL PERSPECTIVE (MATTHEW/MARK/LUKE)

The beginnings of Judaism are rooted in the Judean exiles and their return to their pre-exilic homeland. The experience of the exile and their return mark a change in the central symbols of Israel, hence in marriage strategy as well. The accounts of the return in the books of Ezra and Nehemiah indicate that part of the returning exiles, in order to fit into the prevailing society of Judea, divorced their wives and married into local families.[4] Such behaviour according to Malina, on the part of both the families occupying the land and the returnees was a mutual conciliatory gesture.[5] The book of Malachi sets the tone for this period in the area of marriage strategy, with its instance that what God desires is 'godly offspring'.

In the circumstances addressed by Malachi, what God hates is the divorce of Jew and Jew; there is silence about the divorce of Jew and non-Jew. However, the reform of Ezra requires the divorce of all foreign wives and their children acquired by the returning exiles. Thus, due to the priestly reform of post-exilic Yahwism and its demand for fidelity to the covenant, the marriage strategy worked out in Ezra-Nehemiah, leads to a *'defensive strategy'* - *i.e.* females born within the covenant are to be kept, and entanglement with foreign women are to be resolutely avoided (Ezra 9-10 & Nehemiah 13:23-31).[6]

The implications of the defensive strategy are that the newly formed, closed Jewish community was led to monogamy. Further, the prohibition of divorce as proclaimed by Malachi is antipolygamy in its effects, whether polygamy is successive or simultaneous. It is this defensive marriage strategy coupled with the perception that embeds female sexual purity in male honour that lies at the bottom of the sexual behaviour found in the Priestly writings of the *Old Testament.* These gradually are developed by *'tradition'* into the norms of the first century Palestine. The laws from the previous strategy, as well as the customs of the patriarchal stories, have to be reshaped to fit the new strategy.[7] The earlier creation story of Genesis 2:4ff, is prefaced by a priestly creation story in which God's first command to man is increase and multiply (Genesis 1:28), which is in line with the defensive marriage strategy set out in the rest of the priestly writings.

The holiness code of the priestly tradition is a purity code, a set of explicitly formulated social lines that are to clearly mark the Jews from the non-Jews. This set of boundaries was replicated in the temple structure, in sacrifice procedures, and for our purposes, in sexual behaviour.[8] The general principle is that everything is forbidden unless it fits within the designated social spaces. Legislation specified the designated social spaces. Early Israelite customs on forbidden sexual relationships are restated as incest lines of prohibited degrees of marriage in Leviticus 18:6-18, 20:11-12, 14, 20. Adultery is not only an outrage to male honour, but also an abomination (Leviticus 18:20, 20:10).[9] Sexual hospitality (Leviticus 19:29), keeping Israelite women as slave-wives (Leviticus 25:44-46), priestly marriages with once embedded or shamed women (Leviticus 21:7, 13-14) are not simply affronts to male honour, but equally abominations before the Lord. Since the holy seed or holy offspring are paramount symbols, genealogies tracing holy seed come to have emphatic symbolic importance (*cf* Ezra and Nehemiah).

Perhaps, the most information about the customs of defensive strategy is to be found in Ecclesiasticus, the book of Sirach, who wrote about 150 BC in Jerusalem.[10] According to Sirach, the fathers arranged the marriage (Ecclesiasticus 7:25). In the Hebrew and Syriac text of Ecclesiasticus 7:23, the father is told: *'do you have sons? Correct them and choose wives for them while they are young.'* These points to the practice of early, arranged marriages in which the father engages the girl for his son. In his advice to married men in 9:1-9, Sirach offers counsel on attitudes towards various classes of women. The married man ought to avoid unmarried women because of penalties that might be exacted, presumably by her brothers and father (9:5), and married women ensnare a man in the vengeance of their husbands (9:8-9).[11] Prostitutes lead to a loss of inheritance, either because the offspring would remain fatherless or because the man's father would be shamed by his son's actions (9:6).

Sirach views the wife as embedded in her husband, since divorce means *'to cut her off from your flesh'* (25:26). This is a further indication that marriage is considered a sort of blood relationship, resulting in one flesh.[12] Ecclesiasticus 25:16, 26:27, discuss the ranges of wifely behaviour from shameful to honourable, including rival wives. An important cultural value is alluded by Sirach in Ecclesiaticus 25:21, where the ideal wife is one who is beautiful and wealthy. However, by means of marriage, the wealth of the female passes to the male, *'there is wrath and impudence and great disgrace when a wife supports her husband'* (Ecclesiasticus 25:22). The story of the younger Tobit indicates his proper social placement, since Sarah belongs to his patriline then her wealth belongs to him should he marry her (Tobit 6:11).

As mentioned above, the father is all too vulnerable through his daughters (Ecclesiasticus 26:10-12 and especially 42:9-11). Hence, the cultural imperative to marry them off as soon as possible, which means shortly after the onset of menstruation.[13] Because they are embedded in the male, women can easily shame their fathers and their husbands. Thus, *'better is the wickedness of a man than a women who does good, for it is a woman who brings shame and disgrace'* (Ecclesiasticus 42:14).

This defensive marriage strategy stands as the basic perspective and chief mode of perception for the discussions of marital and sexual behaviour in the Qumran writings, the writings of the early rabbis, as well as the reactions of Jesus recorded in Matthew, Mark and Luke. In the non-legal texts of the period, like Ecclesiasticus, Tobit, and Judith, a person's intentions, his heart, counts in sexual encounters. The focus of this intention in marriage is on offspring, on holy seed, this being the sole valid motivating factor in sexual encounters. Any lesser motives are shameful. Thus, Tobit's wedding night sexual union with Sarah is motivating not by her wealth and beauty, but by the holy seed (Tobit 8:7).

Likewise, in early rabbinic Judaism, marriage entered into because of the beauty or wealth of the bride is equivalent to immorality. The offspring of such marriages are almost tantamount to *bastards,*[14] the symbolic opposite of holy seed. Thus, given this emphasis on defensive strategy and holy seed, imputations of doubtful lineage are among the gravest insults in the culture. For example, John the Baptist calling the Pharisees and the Sadducees of Jerusalem a *'brood of vipers'* (Matthew 3:7, Luke 3:7, Jesus uses the term according to Matthew 12:34, 23:33) means nothing less than *'snake bastards'* a doubly offensive term.[15] Similarly, in Matthew 12:29 and Mark 8:38, Jesus calls his contemporaries an adulterous generation, literally a generation of *bastards* - *i.e.* the offspring of adulterous unions. These are powerful insults in a culture where purity of lineage is a central concern. Jesus' parable on divorce, with re-marriage called adultery, likewise implies *bastard* offspring in such a union (Mark 10:11, Matthew 5:32, 19:19 and Luke 16:18). Jesus' teachings on divorce will be considered below in the rhetorical criticism approach to the relevant texts.

Now we might characterize the post-exilic, Jewish period as focused on the symbol of holy offspring. These holy offspring form a holy people, headed by priests, with worship in the central Temple in the central pre-industrial city. Norms for the period derive from priestly law that covers the behaviour of the priests and non-priest alike. When we turn to the *New Testament* and the typically Christian marriages developed in early Christian communities, we find that they are in most respect continuations of the defensive strategy of Judaism.

A LITERARY CONTEXT OF THE GOSPELS: MATTHEW/MARK/LUKE

In order for the early Christians to communicate with their contemporaries it was essential that they use not only the languages of that era, but also the literary forms and common patterns of oral expression that were then in use. According to Kee, inevitably they did not merely take over these forms unchanged, but adapted them to serve the particular purposes of that particular movement.[16] Since Christianity quickly took root among people of diverse backgrounds, the literary and oral modes of expression were different from place to place in the early Christian world. In both Judaism and Greco-Roman culture of this period, a popular form of communication was the short story about a remarkable public figure.

It might concentrate on some significant action of that person or report a saying or verbal exchange with an antagonist, a pupil or an inquirer. These biographical anecdotes, which compromise much of the Gospels and the Acts, are to be found in the early rabbinic material as well as in accounts of wandering teachers and philosophers of the period. The stories were originally told randomly, in situations in which the content was appropriate. The Gospel tradition eventually linked the stories together in a narrative sequence.[17]

THE GOSPEL ACCORDING TO MATTHEW

Plot

Matthew employs the same basic plot as Mark:—

(a) Jesus' baptism and initial ministry in Galilee
(b) Peter's confession at Caesarea Philippi and the transfiguration
(c) Journey to Jerusalem and debates in the temple
(d) Concluding tragic death and resurrection.

However, Matthew is not a simple repeat of Mark's story. Matthew launches his Gospel with a genealogy and birth narrative that shows Jesus to be the son of David and thus both king and the anointed. This stands in contrast to Mark who starts with John the Baptist preaching. The Gospel concludes with the author appending a commission scene in which the risen Jesus sends the eleven out to baptize the whole world.

Author

According to the early church tradition the author of the Gospel was the apostle Matthew. Papias, one of the early authorities of the church (about 150 CE) claimed that Matthew organized the sayings in the Hebrew language, but scholars have translated them as best as they could.[18] Papias knew the Gospel of Matthew only in its current form and had not seen a version in a Semitic language. Even though later church authorities accepted Papias' assertions, modern scholars have rejected them for various reasons. Firstly, there is no evidence that the Gospel was originally composed in Hebrew. It is written in Koine Greek of the period.[19] Also taking into consideration that it is dependent on Mark, which existed only in Greek. Finally, the Gospel is not a collection of sayings, but a narrative with an ordered plot. Therefore, to refer to the author as Matthew is only a convention.

Date and Community

The first quotation of Matthew; is found in the writing of Ignatius (AD 115), therefore, it is generally agreed that it was written some years preceding Ignatius' writing.[20] A decision about the earliest date at which it could have been written depends upon its relationship to Mark. If Matthew is dependent upon Mark in its present form and Mark was published after Peter's death, than Matthew must clearly be dated later than the above date. A second factor is its relationship to the fall of Jerusalem in AD 70. Some scholars have argued that the Gospel must be dated before AD 70, for it would have been strange for Matthew not to make reference to the destruction of the temple if it had occurred.[21] On the other hand, the indirect reference to the fall of Jerusalem suggests a date after AD 70. Such an argument according to Guthrie and Motyer loses much of its force and its basic assumption that Jesus could not have predicted such an event. It is, therefore, wiser to say that Matthew should be dated somewhere between AD 65 and AD 110, in consideration with the Jewish nature of the Gospel and its many parallels with the Dead Sea Scrolls.[22]

The Matthean community that emerges from a study of the Gospel is engaged in intense debate with rabbinic Judaism that is itself creating new institutions to replace the destroyed temple. Both groups are trying to define themselves. The destruction of Jerusalem set in motion for Judaism and Christianity a long process of consolidation and self-definition that reached its first definitive form around the beginning of the third century.[23] In Judaism this process received a powerful impetus with the triumph of Pharisaism and rabbinic Judaism. Therefore, according to Miller, the rejection of the Pharisees in Matthew implies neither thc rejection of Judaism nor the Law. Even though the Pharisees sit in the chair of Moses (23:2), the standard epithet for them is '*imposters*'. Matthew portrays Jesus as the true and authoritative interpreter of the Law.

Use of Scripture

At important moments in the story the narrator quotes from the scriptures, using the standard formula, *'all this has happened so that the prediction of the Lord given by the Prophet would come true'* (1:22, 2:15, 18, 23, 25). Normally such citations are employed to resolve conflict in the story. Matthew changes certain items in Mark's stories to make the narrative fit the quotations. Matthew's use of quotations from scripture is a guide to the distinctive features of the Matthean Gospel.

Self-portrait

The author has left what seems to be a self-portrait in 13:52 *'every scholar who is schooled in Heaven's imperial rule is like some proprietors who produce from his storeroom treasures old and new'*. This suggests how the Matthean community understood itself: it pores over the records of the past, the scriptures, but it produces something new and original - a new understanding of the Law. The scholar plays an important role in this community. Jesus is regularly pictured as teaching. However, although scholarship and teaching is important to this community Jesus is addressed only by the outsiders as *'Teacher'* or *'Rabbi'*. The disciples and believers refer to him as *'Master'* or *'Lord'*.

THE GOSPEL ACCORDING TO MARK

Story, Structure and Narrative Themes

In this context we start with Jesus and his small band of disciples moving through the little towns, barren countryside, and stormy lake that make up the Gospels controlling landscape. The sense of inevitable confrontation and foreboding grows stronger and stronger. Opposition to his practices and disciples confronts him from social and religious leaders, both those in Galilee and others summoned from Jerusalem (e.g. 3:19-22, 7:1-21). Two dominant themes throughout the Gospel are (a) identity, and (b) the nature of discipleship.

Origins of the Gospel

The document itself never mentions its author, place, time or circumstances of its origin. However, scholars have inferred that the Gospel was composed at about the time of the Roman-Judean War (66-70 CE), in the Greek speaking Syria.[24] The traditional name 'Mark' is used as a convenient way to refer to the anonymous writer. The actual name and gender of the author is unknown.

If we relate Mark as being the first Gospel, then its predecessors would not have been evangelist in the literary sense, instead prophets, teachers, missionaries, or community organizers who passed along memories and stories of Jesus in their own particular social and church situations.[25] According to Miller, Mark drew on many sorts of existing material for his own new purposes of narration.[26] However, identifying Mark's sources and judging whether they were available in written or oral forms make a difficult enterprise.

Notes on Mark's Narrative Style

Mark uses a lively and direct storyteller's style. The Greek prose employed is the informal language of ordinary men and women who made up the common Eastern Mediterranean culture in the first century. Evident in the Gospel is an immediacy and simplicity of description; a certain harshness and awkwardness in expression; repetition of favoured words and constructions; and sketchiness in characterization. Thus, Mark's story is close stylistically and historically to the oral environment.

Expansions in Mark's Text

During the process of copying and re-copying Mark's Gospel, the scribes introduced some major expansions into the text. It seems as though the scribes were unsatisfied with the conclusion showing the terrified women running from the tomb (16:8) that they preferred to continue with editions of various lengths to portray the risen Jesus appearing to his disciples and commanding them to begin the work of evangelization. These additions are traditionally called *'shorter ending'* and *'longer ending'* of Mark, though it would be more appropriate according to Miller, to term them '*shorter/longer supplements.*'[27] Most of this material is closely patterned on other post-resurrection appearance stories, especially those in Luke's Gospel.

THE GOSPEL ACCORDING TO LUKE

Luke's Narrative

The Books Luke and Acts, comprise over one-fourth of the total text of the *New Testament.* The narrative begins in Jerusalem before the birth of Jesus and ends with Paul preaching the Gospel in Rome. Luke sets the story of Jesus within the larger story - *i.e.* God's plan to offer salvation to humankind. However, according to Miller, in Luke unlike the other Gospels, Jesus is not the prime mover of the narrative, though he is the central figure.[28] It is God who determines the course of events in the story. Luke expresses this by describing certain events as predetermined (*e.g.* 2:25, 22:22, Acts 2:23, 4:27-28) or directed by the Holy Spirit (*e.g.* 3:22, 4:1, 14, 18, 12:12). Although, God directs the story, He does so from '*off-stage*'. God speaks directly only twice to certify the divine mandate of Jesus' mission (3:22, 9:35).

Luke's Portrait of Jesus

These two divine interventions in the narrative underline the fundamental aspect of Luke's portrayal of Jesus: *(a)* He is the divinely commissioned agent who announces and promotes God's will for Israel. In his first public speech (4:16-30), Jesus predicts that his mission will fulfil the words of the prophets and will meet the same reception as the prophets met before him. *(b)* The second central aspect of Luke's portrayal of Jesus is his solicitude for the poor and the outcast. Jesus claims that his outreach to them constitutes his messianic credentials (7:18-22).

Structure

The Gospel is not a tightly structured narrative. Luke derives his basic story outline from the Gospel of Mark:

1. John the Baptist setting the stage for Jesus.
2. Jesus' baptism, temptation, announcement of his message, and gathering of disciples.
3. Teaching and healing in Galilee.
4. Journey to Jerusalem, culminating in a symbolic action in the temple.
5. Preaching in the temple, culminating in an eschatological discourse.
6. Arrest, trial and crucifixion.
7. Discovery of the empty tomb.

Luke also expands the journey to Jerusalem, making it a major vehicle for his exposition of Jesus' teachings.[29]

Luke's Audience

The Gospel of Luke illustrates a strong interest in the universalism of the Christian message. Luke's writing shows sensitivity for a Gentile audience. According to Miller, Luke regularly translates or omits Aramaic terms in his sources, and often submits Greek names for Semiotic ones.[30] Luke omits Mark's story of the Syro-Phoenician woman (Mark 7:24-30), the one story that would most likely offend Gentiles. He depicts Jesus freely interacting with non-Jews and uses them as positive examples in his teachings (4:25-27, 7:1-10, 10: 29-37; 17:11-19).

Luke also presents Jesus to be intelligible to the Greco-Roman readers.[31] He sets Jesus' birth in the context of world history (2:1) and traces his genealogy (3:23-38) all the way to Adam (not simply to the Jewish progenitor Abraham, as in the genealogy offered by Matthew). Although Luke affirms that Jesus is the Jewish Messiah foretold in the scriptures (4:21), Luke is the only synoptic writer to present Jesus also as a *'savior'* (2:11, Acts 3:13-15), a Hellenistic title for divine deliverers.

APPLICATION OF RHETORICAL CRITICISM TO MATTHEW/MARK AND LUKE

After providing a social, historical and literary background to the texts of the Synoptic Gospels - *i.e.* Matthew, Mark and Luke, we will now attempt an application of rhetorical criticism to the relevant texts concerning the ethical discourse of divorce between Jesus and the Pharisees.

Rhetorical Unit/s

The Macro-Rhetorical Unit/s

The macro-rhetorical unit is the ethical discourse between Jesus and the religious leaders (*i.e.* the Pharisees). After having shown something of the life, which will be possible within the Messianic community, the Messiah according to Matthew began his journey from Galilee to Jerusalem to present to the holy city and the Jewish leaders the challenge to become the centre and nucleus of the renewed people of God.[32] There is an atmosphere of crisis for the men must decide about Jesus and their decision is connected with temporal and eternal judgement. In the course of Jesus' journey we find an ethical confrontation between Jesus and the Pharisees. This section of Matthew 19:1-12 is parallel to Mark 10:1-16, with an addition of the saying about celibacy (vv. 10-12). The discourse is also referred in Luke 16:18 concerning the Pharisees and the law. These parallels form the macro-rhetorical unit, which is a confrontation between Jesus and the Pharisees concerning divorce.

The Micro-Rhetorical Unit/s

Within the macro-rhetorical unit/s of the divorce discourse in Matthew 19:1-12, Mark 10:1-12 and Luke 16:18, we have a further division into three micro-rhetorical units. Rhetorical unit 1 is a combination of Matthew 19:1-2 and Mark 10:1, which forms the discourse introduction. The climax of the narrative is the actual discourse/an argumentative dialogue between Jesus and the Pharisees in rhetorical unit 2, which is composed of Matthew 19:3-9, Mark 10:2-9 and Luke 16:18. The narrative ends with the third rhetorical unit, which is the dialogue between Jesus and his disciples, Matthew 19:10-12 and Mark 10:10-12.

The following is an analysis of the divorce discourse of the Synoptic Gospels within its respective rhetorical units.

Rhetorical Unit 1: Discourse Introduction

Matthew 19:1-2

According to Hill, in rhetorical unit 1, we find an application of the usual sentence, *'Now it came to pass when Jesus had finished his sayings'* (19:1), which ends the discourse (*cf* 7:28, 11:1, 13:53, 26:1), and marks the end of the fourth main section of the Gospel and the beginning of the fifth (19:3-26:2).[33] Jesus leaves Galilee to go to Perea on his way to Jerusalem. This common route from Galilee to Jerusalem avoided Samaria. The region east of the Jordan, ruled by Herod Antipas, was called Perea. Its inhabitants were largely Jews.[34] The crowds that followed Jesus were either going to the Passover, as Jesus and his disciples, or coming to Jesus for help.[35] The hyperbole *'healed them'* literally implies that all were sick and were healed. To Jesus and Matthew, the healing attested the beginning of the Kingdom.[36]

Mark 10:1

In verse 1 *'went to the region of Judea, and beyond Jordan'*, Mark reverses the order envisaged elsewhere in his texts. In other scenes Mark portrays Jesus has travelling along the east bank of Jordan, and then into Judea. The question that emerges is whether this reverse is a simple relic of an old tradition underlying Mark at this point. Or has Mark himself put Judea first, to emphasize Jesus' set intent, after the passion prediction of 9:30-32, to advance to Jerusalem to his death? According to Anderson, whatever the origin of the reverse designation, and however, Mark may have pictured Jesus' journey, his primary interests lie in the geography than in those favorite motives of his - *i.e.* the magnetic attraction of Jesus (crowds gathered to him again) and the good news he brings through his teachings.[37]

Rhetorical Unit 2: Ethical Discourse – Jesus' Confrontation with the Pharisees

Matthew 19: 3-9

Rhetorical unit 2 is the actual confrontation between Jesus and the

Pharisees concerning the issue of divorce. In 19:3, the problem of divorce, which had been touched upon in the Sermon on the Mount (5:23), is now dealt with in the context of a debate/discourse between Jesus and the Pharisees. According to Filson, the Pharisees were present to observe Jesus, hear his teachings and test him.[38] In 19:3, we find that the Pharisees challenge Jesus with the question: *'Is it lawful for a man to divorce his wife for just any reason?'* The Pharisees had long disputed over the meaning of Deuteronomy 24:1. They agreed that the text permitted divorce. However, they differed over the meaning of *'some indecency'*. According to the strict school of Rabbi Shammai, divorce was limited to immorality by the wife. However, the more liberal view of Rabbi Hillel, said that it referred to anything in/of the wife that displeased the husband.[39]

In 19:4-6, we find a response of Jesus to the challenge posed to him by the Pharisees. Jesus responds with the question *'Have you not read?'* He shifts the focus of the discourse to Scripture. He starts his response to the challenge by quoting Genesis 1:27 that God had created man and woman to live together in a monogamous marriage. Jesus then cites Genesis 2:24, a man is to leave his parents and unite with his bride in a union so complete that they are no longer two independent individuals, but one flesh. They now resemble a new creation that has its life only in their union. God has made them one. The husband must not break by divorce this permanent monogamous union. A reference is made to the husband, because according to Jewish law, only the man could legitimize a divorce by giving the woman a written certificate of divorce. In the response of Jesus to the Pharisees challenge we find that Jesus leaves no room for divorce.

In 19:7, we find a counter challenge by the Pharisees to the response of Jesus. The Pharisees appeal to Deuteronomy 24:1 arguing that Moses clearly sanctions divorce. In 19:8, Jesus responds to the Pharisees counter challenge by stating that Moses permitted divorce only in view of the hardness of man's heart. Divorce is wrong, a right attitude would avoid it and fulfil the creator's purpose and will.[40]

The most notable Matthean feature is the addition of the exceptive phrase in 19:9, an exception that also appears in Matthew 5:32. In 19:9, there is recognition of the one valid ground for divorce *'unchastity'* (*i.e.* adultery or some other marital unfaithfulness, rather than marriage within the prohibited degree) on the part of the woman.

By the addition of the clause *'for any cause'* (19:3), to the Gospel of Mark, Matthew has brought the question of divorce into the realm of strict legal discussion.[41] However, to allow divorce for every kind of unchastity would seem to nullify the force of the prohibition. Some interpret the exception to refer to adultery and so permit divorce and re-marriage of the innocent party in a marriage where the other was an adulterer.[42]

However, its treatment, like that of Mark, cannot be interpreted as a radical departure from the Law of Moses, but only as a radical interpretation of the Law. It should also be noted that Genesis 1:27 to which Matthew appeals is also a part of the written Law.[43] This form of argumentation employed was acceptable in Jewish exegesis: 'the more original the weightier'; an appeal to God's intention in creation outweighs (but does not annul) the ordinances of Moses.[44]

According to Filson, *verse* 9 makes Jesus agree with the teachings of Shammai against Hillel.[45] However, the crux of Jesus' debate is that God intends man and woman to live together in a permanent monogamous union. It has been argued that Matthew gives the implied meaning of Jesus, who said nothing of the exception clause, but assumed that the actual immorality on the part of the wife would break the union and warrant divorce.[46] Since, Jesus' primary objective was to state and defend the permanent nature of true marriage; we can assume that Matthew adapted his teaching to support the stricter line of Jewish teaching. An adulterous relationship violated the order of creation, with its monogamous ideal. However, if Jesus upheld the indissolubility of marriage on the basis of Genesis, He must have permitted divorce for adulterous marriages, which contravened the created order.[47]

According to Guthrie and Motyer, the moral principal of monogamy is clearly stated in this rhetorical unit. However, there is no reason to suppose that civil legislation should not permit divorce in cases where the ideal has not been attained.[48]

Mark 10: 2-9

The second rhetorical unit is focused only on putting Jesus to the test or trying to trap him. The Pharisees appear in this rhetorical unit as representatives of those who do not come to Jesus with genuine openness, but have made up their minds before they could give him a chance. This would imply a hidden agenda or ulterior motif. In consideration of Anderson's analysis, certain ancient versions of Mark omit Pharisees and leave unspecified the subject of the verb *asked*, and possible the original text did not name the questioners of Jesus.[49] However, the question posed, could not have come from any group of Jews, since a man's legal right to divorce his wife, was everywhere accepted on the basis of Deuteronomy 24:1. However, noted above in rhetorical unit 2 of Matthew 19, the two schools of rabbinic thought did discuss the meaning of the phrase *'indecent thing'*. Therefore, the question put in verse 2, to whether it is lawful for a man to divorce his wife, is a church or Marcan formulation leading up to the teaching in verses 6-9.[50]

In verse 3, Jesus answers his opponents with a counter question, which puts them on the spot by forcing them to reckon with God's will for them as it is expressed in the commandment of the Law. The reply with reference to Deut. 24:1 was that Moses allowed divorce, provided that certain legal formalities designed to protect the divorced woman were carried through. In considering verses 5ff, the reply of the Pharisees together with the original question in verse 2 *' Is a man allowed?'* shows that they reckon less with God's will for them than with their own rights within the limit of what is permitted.

In reply Jesus first pointed out that Moses' legislation was a concession to human weakness and rightly introduced to regulate divorce in a defective state of society. When Jesus said *'for the hardness of your heart, he wrote you this commandment'*, he is neither here or in what follows overthrowing Scripture, nor setting God's command against that of Moses. Rather, he makes it clear that in adopting Deut. 24:1 as their starting point, his interlocutors mistakenly suppose that first and foremost God approves divorce, whereas this commandment of the Law is no concession to human weakness but stands as divine judgement on man's 'impenetrable stubbornness and obtuseness in regard to what is God's true will for them'.[51]

In verses 6ff, Jesus appeals from Scripture to Scripture, to the only real starting-point, namely *'what God has intended from the beginning'*. The phrase *'from the beginning'*, is an appeal of how things may be from the human point of view in respect of the Law concerning divorce to how things are in the order of God's creation.[52] Jesus' standpoint is itself founded on Scripture, Genesis 1:27: *God made them male and female.* In creating two sexes, God declared his intention that one man is for one woman.[53] In Genesis 2:24, *'for this reason'*, refers back to the creation of the woman out of Adam's rib, but here it is applied to the statement of Genesis 1:27, which is interpreted as a sign that the union between one man and one woman in marriage was ordained by God to transcend all other human ties and relationships.

The argument of Jesus is that in accordance with God's will, marriage is the closest conceivable bond *'two shall become one'*. Verse 9 *'what therefore God has joined...asunder'*, sums up the position stated by Jesus in the plainest possible way. Whatever a man may say or do, or whatever proceedings he may take, he remains inescapable under the absolute command, will, and authority of God in creation. However, it is most important to remember that in Mark 10:6-9, Jesus is not absolutely prohibiting divorce *by way of a binding legal enactment,*[54] but is elevating marriage (as an indissoluble union) by way of leading men to understand it, not as a remote ideal, but as a gift of God's creation, to be received gladly and celebrated.

Luke 16:18

Luke 16:18 fits into rhetorical unit 3 with the confrontation of Jesus and the Pharisees. However, we will focus only on the response to divorce. Technically the law allowed divorce. But divorce was contrary to its intent as seen above. This is an example of how the true purpose of the law had continuing validity in the Kingdom of God. Luke 16:18 presents an antidote to the anti-nominal attitude, which argued that the message of Jesus made the *Old Testament* law and its morals insignificant. However, Jesus stated that this was not so, and that men would find God's will still expressed in the *Old Testament* (*Vs.* 29). The era of the law and the prophets had ended, and now the era of the New Kingdom had come, but this did not mean that the law had been countermanded. In retrospect, it implied that the era of the New Kingdom meant the establishment of Kingdom ethics.

For example, divorce followed by re-marriage is adultery. This particular example sharpened the law, the Jews thought of adultery as a sin by a woman against her husband or by one man against another.

However, Jesus taught that a man also commits adultery against a woman.[55]

Rhetorical Unit 3: Jesus' Dialogue with the Disciples

Matthew 19:10-12

In rhetorical unit 3, we find a dialogue between Jesus and His disciples. Verses 10-12 are a dialogue concerning the self-consecration for the sake of the Kingdom of God. Voluntary celibacy was extremely rare among the Jews, but in the Essene (*i.e.* Qumran community) it was very highly regarded.[56] Abstinence from marital and sexual relations may have been obligatory on all full priestly members of the sect under the law of the eschatological war. A recent study of this pericope argues that Jesus like the Qumran community was intensely aware of living in the end of the Age. He was conscious of being the fulfilment of the promise of a New Temple, within which his disciples would live, like priests, after the rules (on marriage) in Ezekiel 44:22. Thus, the sayings of Jesus, reproduce Jesus' use of Isaiah 56:4-5, where the eunuch's fidelity to the covenant is more important as a sign of his incorporation in the New Temple worship than to contribute offspring to the community.[57]

Verse 10 links the teaching on marriage and divorce with further teaching. Since marriage was almost a duty to the Jew, the disciples are represented as thinking that to have such firm restrictions around divorce makes marriage disadvantageous or unwelcome. They are virtually making the attractiveness of marriage contingent upon the possibility of easy divorce.[58]

In verse 11, the reply of Jesus indicated that not everybody can receive and put into practice the precept of abstinence, not all are capable of living by the above principle, but only those who are fitted for and called to it: *'He who is able to receive this, let him receive it.'* In verse 12, those to whom celibacy is given are those that are born impotent, those made impotent by physical means, and those who have voluntary renounced marriage in order to devote all their time and energies to the service of the Kingdom. The expression '*eunuchs by men'* is a well-known rabbinical phrase: 'eunuchs for...the kingdom of heaven' could be original to Jesus. According to Hill, Essene

Judaism may have provided the spiritual milieu, which nurtured the ideal of a self-consecration to a holy life and warfare, which included celibacy (*cf* 1 Cor. 7:7).[59] Not everyone can practice that state, but it is difficult to avoid the impression that by implication the celibate is exalted above the married.

Mark 10:10-12

The setting of the scene in verses 10-12 - *i.e.* '*in the house*' provides the customary Marcan transition from public pronouncement of Jesus to private communication.[60] In this rhetorical unit, we find that the disciples still do not understand the teaching of Jesus, and the fact that further special instruction is offered to them, indicates how strong is Jesus' desire to get across to them the ethics of the Kingdom. No doubt Mark considered the saying(s) of verses 11-12 an endorsement of Jesus' public teaching on marriage (10:6-9). However, these verses are so only indirectly, and in fact relate less to divorce than to re-marriage, which is condemned as a grievous sin for divorced persons.

In verse 11, the normal Jewish view according to rabbinic law, was that a man could be said to commit adultery against another married man, and a wife could be held to commit adultery against her husband, but a husband could not be held to commit adultery against his wife.[61] According to Jewish Law, only the man had the right to divorce his wife, at this point the statement of verse 11 is thoroughly Jewish. However, the continuation of the verse represents a dramatic departure from Jewish norms in claiming that the man who has divorced his wife, and re-married commits adultery against his wife. The saying of verse 11 has a parallel in Matthew 5:32 and Luke 16:18.

According to Jewish law, a wife had no right to divorce her husband. Therefore, the statement of verse 12 can hardly have a Jewish background. Roman law, however, gave the woman her right to divorce her husband, and so in verse 12 we may see the Hellenistic Church accommodating the older and more Jewish statement of verse 11 to new circumstances and new relationships.[62] According to Anderson, the sayings of verses 11-12 appear to be legal in character, it is very doubtful whether in their present form they can be traced back to Jesus.[63] This is substantiated by the fact that Jesus' public teaching (verses 6-9) is opposed to and transcends every kind of legal regulation.

Relational Posture of the Rhetorical Unit/s

In an analysis of the relational posture of the rhetorical units of Matthew, Mark and Luke, we will examine how the text chooses to relate itself to its readers/audience. In the analysis we will focus on the modalities assumed and the deixis.

Modalities

In the exegesis of the Ezra and Nehemiah texts, we noted that modalities had an important function in controlling the presentation - *i.e.* the relationship asserted within the argument fostering the implementation of divorce. In the ethical discourse concerning divorce, in Matthew, Mark and Luke, these modalities emerge once again to direct the presentation to counter the implementation of divorce. These emerging modalities modify the reality of the discourse between Jesus and the Pharisees, and operate within the text's intentionality, as well as in the audience. In turning to the text and analyzing how it chooses to relate itself to the audience, we find that the modalities assumed are:

Highly Argumentative: The text asserts itself as a methodological reasoning distinguishing between what is ethical (*i.e.* Jesus and the Kingdom ethics) and what is non-ethical (*i.e.* Pharisees and secular ethics) in the context of the law concerning divorce.

Communicative: Although the text functions in a highly argumentative modality it is also communicative. An understanding of the discourse and its elements is transmitted to its audience.

Coherent: The text is communicative due to it being coherent. This is due to the consistency of propositions employed by the writer as a technique to create a consistent narrative of the discourse surrounding the issue of divorce.

Active: In considering the genre of the texts as a narrative discourse, the text is active. With its practical elements and interpretation of the law in the discourse the audience becomes active participants of the narrative - *i.e.* they identify with either Jesus or the Pharisees as an expression of their perceptions concerning the issue of divorce and the interpretation of the law.

Assertive: The text then becomes assertive - *i.e.* compelling the audience to understand the discourse as being that of Kingdom ethics in contrast to secular ethics of the Pharisees. The interpretation of Jesus then becomes assertive as the ethical norms to be followed.

Injunctive: In order for the texts to be assertive, it must be injunctive. Injunctive implying authoritative. This authority is asserted through the ethical understanding of Jesus being the ethics affirmed and held by the writer.

However, for these specific forms of modalities to function in this interaction (text and audience), there must be a set of conditions provided by a background or context determined by the author's and reader's skill in communication, which is based on their shared norms, social values, desires and the communicant's belief and knowledge.

In the analysis, we find that there are two major modals among the major argumentative units. These modals are similar to that of Ezra and Nehemiah: (i) Cognitional Mode and (ii) Volitional Mode.

Cognitional Mode

In the Gospel of Matthew 19:3, we find that there is a common understanding between the author and the audience surrounding the two major schools of interpretation on the subject of divorce among the Jewish rabbis. The author and audience also share a common understanding of the Scriptures relating to the original creation narrative (19:4-6). There is also a common understanding to the institution of divorce and its procedure. A divorce could only be legitimized if a certificate of divorce is issued to the wife. In Matthew we also find that the author and audience both share the belief in the exception clause, which highlights the purgatory of adultery as being an abomination to the marriage union and God (19:9). The author and audience also share a common understanding of the existence of the institution of celibacy (19:11-12) that was prevalent in that society. This implies the sharing of common commitment to the known tradition of the prevailing institutions of marriage and divorce.

In Mark 10:1-12, we also find similarities that are shared with Matthew and his audience. In 10:4, we find a shared social reference system to the institution of divorce compelling a man to write a certificate of divorce, which legitimized the process of divorce. In 10:5-9, we find a reference to the creative narrative which both the audience and author shared - *i.e.* knowledge of the divine institution of marriage. It is suffice to say that the divine ideal (10:6-9) can be interpreted as endorsing the Mosaic concession (which is shared by the author and audience), yet to the disciples it moves on a higher level at which undoubtedly the individual believer must reckon.

In considering the principle of Malina and Rohrbaugh, there is a greater dimension of the social perspective of divorce that needs to be explored within the cognitional mode of the texts.[64] For an understanding of divorce (between the author and the audience), one must understand what marriage meant to this specific community. Under normal circumstances in the world of Jesus, individuals did not really get married rather families did. Thus, in first century Mediterranean World and earlier, marriage symbolized the fusion of the honour of two extended families and was undertaken with a view to political, and/or economic concerns – even when it might be confined to fellow ethnics, as in first century Israel.[65] Divorce then would entail the dissolution of family ties, a challenge to the family of the former wife, and feuding.

According to the authors of the synoptic texts, Jesus looked upon the married couple as *'no longer two, but one flesh'*. This indicated that marriage was a blood relationship rather than a legal one. As a blood relationship is between mother and father and the children, marriage cannot be legally dissolved. In the community (*i.e.* audience) of Matthew/Mark/Luke, what is prohibited is divorce and re-marriage, or divorce in order to re-marry. Divorce due to the above reasons will inevitably lead to family feuding, a true negative challenge to the honour of the former wife's family.[66] However, in the community of Matthew/Mark/Luke, in cases of adultery, divorce was in order. According to Malina and Rohrbaugh, the prohibition of adultery in the Ten Commandments was intended to reduce chances of endless feuding in Israel.[67] Adultery required a male to defend his own and his family's honour against the offending adulterer.

If a husband divorced his wife in order to re-marry, the father (or other males) of the family of the divorced wife would be dishonoured. In other words, it is the family of the divorced wife, who is dishonoured by her husband's divorcing and marrying another. This leads to family feuding over a status of family honour. As a result, divorce for this reason is prohibited in the synoptic Gospels.

Volitional Mode

In rhetorical unit 2, where we have the confrontation between Jesus and the Pharisees we find that the argument takes place in an atmosphere of judgement. The Pharisees are judging the teachings of Jesus according to their interpretation of Scripture. Jesus in return judges their interpretation against His interpretation. The discourse in rhetorical unit 2, due to its argumentative nature is thus, of authoritative command and judgement. The discourse also functions within a sphere of correction and rebuke. Jesus corrects their misunderstanding of Moses' concession and rebukes, the Pharisees for their selfishness, in twisting the Mosaic Law for their own gain rather than the will of God.

However, in rhetorical unit 3, where Jesus speaks to his disciples, we find that the dialogue still functions within an authoritative command. However, the discourse is not judgmental but rather educative. Jesus in his private explication of divorce (Mark 10:10) is educating the disciples rather than judging their teachings/beliefs. According to Rewers, dialogue is a 'confrontation and interpretation of human utterances within a new context'.[68]

Deixis

In analyzing the content of the text in relationship to time, place and personal participants the following deixis will be examined: (i) Personal Deixis, (ii) Intonational Deixis, (iii) Spatial Deixis, and (iv) Temporal Deixis.

Personal Deixis

An analysis of the personal deixis of the synoptic texts includes an examination of the use of *person and demonstrative pronouns, personal names, and substantives*.

Matthew 19:1-12: In the first rhetorical unit, we have a reference to *'the great multitudes'* that followed Jesus (19:2). In the latter part of the verse, He healed *'them'*. From an analysis of the inclusive term *'them'*, we find that all the people who followed Jesus were in need of his help. In the context of his journey, Jesus is confronted by the Pharisees.

The Pharisees were members of what would soon become an important religious and political movement.[69] They believed that all of the Jewish people should obey the Law. The Pharisees were well educated Jews who sought to extend to its maximum the concept of the holy people of God. The Pharisees believed that the Law included the Torah, the five books of Moses, but also a body of legal interpretations supposedly given first to Moses and then passed down by oral tradition to the present day (*i.e.* Oral Torah).[70] Few peasants could even approach the standards set for them by the Pharisees. A religious leader who identified with the peasantry and who suggested that they might be acceptable to God without detailed concern for the 'Oral Torah' would be opposed by the Pharisees.

Jesus was seen as an opposition to the Pharisees. Jesus taught obedience to the Law, while at the same time he was in conflict with the pharisaic instructors of the Law, who accused him of being in opposition to the Law.[71] This is due to Jesus calling for the obedience to the Law in the books of Moses, but did not require the peasants to obey strict pharisaic interpretations of it. During the time of Jesus, the Pharisees were somewhat influential, but they were a distinct minority. Their power grew enormously during the first century, and by the end of that century, they were the dominant forces in Judaism.[72]

In verse 3, we find that the Pharisees made a challenge to Jesus. In verse 4 when Jesus replies, Matthew focuses Jesus' response to '*them*'. It is obvious that only one person posed the question, however, in Matthew's text we find that Jesus addresses his response to '*them*', a collective term used to denote the social group - *i.e.* the Pharisees as an entity. This is also seen in rhetorical unit 3, where he addresses his disciples as a collective '*them*'.

Mark 10:1-12: In Mark we have a similar deixis as that of Matthew. In verse, a great multitude gathered to him (not followed him as in Matthew), and he taught *'them'* (stands in contrast to Matthew 19:2 where he healed them). In Mark we have the confrontation between Jesus and the dialogue with his disciples. Mark similar to Matthew uses the collective term '*them*' in his response.

In Luke, however, we find that the personal deixis changes. Luke 16: 14 addresses Jesus' response directly to the Pharisees. '*You are those who justify yourself before men...*' In Luke we find that '*you*' is used as an inclusive term for the Pharisees and in the same clause '*yourself'* is used as an exclusive term to set the Pharisaic movement in distinction from the others.

In the context of personal deixis, one should also take into consideration the use of proper names, social groups, types and places.

	Matthew	Mark	Luke
(a) Proper Names			
Jesus	19:1	19:5	
Moses	19:7	19:3-4	
(b) Social Groups			
Pharisees	19:3	10:2	16:14
Disciples	19:10	10:10	16:1
(c) Types			
Great Multitudes	19:2	10:1	
Eunuchs	19:12		
(d) Places			
Judea	19:1	10:1	
Jordan	19:1	10:1	
Galilee	19:1		
In the house		10:10	

Intonational Deixis

In evaluating the intonational deixis of the synoptic texts, we focus on the emotion and the evaluative attitude of the speaker. Matthew 19:3 and Mark 10:2 portray the Pharisees approaching Jesus with an ulterior motive - *i.e. 'testing him'*. In considering the insights of Davies, the Pharisees saw Jesus as an opposition to their interpretation and teaching of the Law.[73] Therefore, it culminated in a test. Matthew and Mark use the phrase *'testing him'* to emphasize the ulterior motif of the Pharisees. In Matthew and Mark there is limited expression of the writers' attitude and emotions surrounding the discourse, however, in Luke we find a more vivid narrative.

The narrative starts in Luke 16:14, where the Pharisees are described as *'the lovers of money'*. Instead of the Pharisees challenging or testing Jesus, Luke uses the verb *'derided'*, which means '*to laugh scornfully'* or '*treat with scorn'*. The writing of Luke exhibits great animosity against the Pharisees this is evident in verse 15, *'you are those who justify yourself before men'*.

Spatial Deixis

Spatial deixis is used with reference to geographical names and places. In rhetorical unit 1, the narrative of Matthew begins with Jesus departing from Galilee and going to the region of Judea beyond Jordan (Matt. 19:1). Mark also begins his narrative with Jesus' journey to the region of Judea by the other side of Jordan (Mark 10:1). The discourse with the Pharisees takes place in the course of Jesus' journey.

The narratives of Matthew and Luke have one setting, whereas in Mark the confrontation of Jesus and the Pharisees occur in the course of his journey, whilst the dialogue with his disciples occur in a house (Mark 10:10).

Temporal Deixis

In Matthew/Mark/Luke, we find temporal deixis present in the context of the understanding of divorce. Set against the ethical codes of what are perceived by the Pharisees as ethically correct, known and valued, the author devaluates the ethics of the Pharisees in response to the ethics of the Kingdom presented by Jesus.

In these texts, we find a tension between the current understanding of divorce and adultery and the future fulfilment of the divine purpose of God's will for mankind. Technically the law allowed divorce (Deut. 24:1). The era of the law and the prophets had ended, and now the era of the New Kingdom had come.

Jews thought of adultery as a sin by a woman against her husband or by one man against another. However, Jesus taught that a man also commits adultery against a woman.[74] This had future implications in marriage and divorce as perceived by the community. The temporal deixis also questioned the legitimization of divorce in contrast to the original divine plan for man and woman - *i.e.* a marriage union where man and woman form *one flesh.*

Method of Argumentation

In analyzing the method of argumentation, two methods of argumentation can be identified, namely *deliberative and epideictic.*

Deliberative

In searching for the actual rhetorical historical situation in which the discourse takes place, this research has combined ancient and modern rhetoric (*i.e.* modern theory of argumentation and discourse theory) in order to ascertain an important difference among the levels of discourse within the text.

The synoptic texts (*i.e.* Matthew 19:1-12, Mark 10:1-12 and Luke 16:18) should be viewed as a deliberative discourse. By *deliberative discourse*, we refer to a discourse of persuasion of the audience to take action for the future, action for its best interest.[75] The goal of this narrative discourse in the context of Matthew, Mark and Luke's community is to prohibit divorce with the intention to re-marry (Matt. 19:9, Mark 10:11, Luke 16:18) and to recognize and subject themselves; to the divine plan of creation (Matt. 19:4-6, Mk 10:4-9). This implied one man for one woman joining to form one flesh. The main issue to be settled between Jesus and the Pharisees; concerns whether it is lawful to divorce a wife (Matt 19:3 '*for any reason*', Mk 10:2).

The first step is to re-construct a 'plausible' historical rhetorical situation in which the discourse might be construed as a fitting response. Debates with the community of Matthew/Mark/Luke take place concerning the social definition of divorce, interpretations of the Mosaic Law, and the Kingdom ethics pronounced by Jesus. As a result of competing interpretations and practices within the two rabbinical schools of Hillel and Shammai, the Pharisees challenge a response from Jesus, to substantiate the view of either one of the prevailing schools of thought. In considering the many confrontations that Jesus has had with the Pharisees and other religious teachers, it is assumed that the competence and lifestyle of Jesus was held in low esteem due to his association with the peasants and the prostitutes. Jesus sets himself as not coming to countermand the Mosaic Law. In order to succeed, he appeals to the Pharisees to turn to the Scriptures and understand God's original divine plan for mankind to make the necessary ethical decisions.

However, because Jesus chooses to address the issue of divorce and re-marriage in a certain deliberative fashion, it does not necessarily imply anything more than a choice on his part regarding effective argumentative strategy. This research proposes a rhetorical interpretation of the discourse as deliberative oratory, and assumes a council-like setting to the historical reconstruction of the relationship between Jesus and the Pharisees. Jesus is seen as one of the 'rabbis' or 'teachers' to the community - *i.e.* the multitudes that followed him (Matt. 19:1-2, Mk. 10:1). However, he is attempting through the proper interpretation of Scripture that the Pharisees subjugate to him as the greater teacher and rightful interpreter of the Law. Once done, he can then involve himself in the deliberation of the community, primarily by authoritative demand.

The argumentative situation can change and develop during the discourse, reflecting strategies and attempts at persuasion, the selection of each being determined by the rhetor's interpretation of the audience's situation.[76] This can be seen in the synoptic texts. Jesus builds upon the interpretation of the texts and God's divine plan for creation to shift his argument to the non-ethical practices of the community - *i.e.* divorce with the intention to remarry.

The argument through its strategy develops a 'context', in which the argument attempts on being effective in influencing the audience to the ethical pragmatism that it demands from them. Jesus has attempted various perspectives in his attempt to convince the Pharisees to act correctly - *i.e.* understand that Moses permitted divorce due to the *hardness of their hearts*, however, the divine plan of God is for one man and one woman to join in marriage union to form a close bond becoming one flesh.

Epideictic

Turning now to the second perspective under consideration, is the view that the texts of the Synoptic Gospels, functions as epideictic or demonstrative discourse, defined by Perelman as '*a discourse which sets out to increase the intensity of adherence to certain values, which might not be contested when considered on their own but may nevertheless prevail against other values that might come into conflict with them*'.[77]

Epideictic focuses on reinforcing a sense of communion between the orator and the audience. It aims towards directing the audience, by every available means, to what is already accepted, and therefore, attempts to obtain not so much a decision to act than a disposition towards action.[78] The writers of the synoptic Gospels do this by means of digressions. Digressions are used to realize/make present an issue for the audience through amplification, example, intensification etc.

Matthew 19:4-6 and Mark 10:5-9 can be identified as a major digression, serving effectively to intensify adherence to the issue at hand. The writers use Jesus' allusion to the creation narrative of God's original designated plan for mankind as an example, which the audience should imitate, as the paradigm of the values lauded. It functions further to increase commitment and the disposition to appropriate action (contrasting that of divorce). Therefore, the writers do not argue concerning whether it is lawful for a man to divorce his wife, but to reinforce the original plan of God.

Shifts in Argumentation

The above section clarifies the shifts evidenced in the argumentative discourse throughout the performance of the narratives.

In Matthew 19:1-12, the narrative begins with Jesus departing from Galilee and going to the region of Judea and healing the multitudes that followed him (19:1-2). The argument then shifts to the Pharisees challenging Jesus, *'Is it lawful for a man to divorce his wife for just any reason?'* (19:3) Jesus responds to this argument by stating the creative narrative and God's original divine plan for mankind (19:4-6). It then shifts to a counter argument from the Pharisees, referring to the command of Moses to issue a certificate of divorce (19:7). This is followed by a counter response from Jesus stating that this was commanded due to the hardness of their hearts. In this argument, we find the introduction of the exception clause. In cases of adultery divorce can be obtained (19:8-9). The argument then shifts to the disciples and their question of whether it is better for a man to marry or consecrate his life as a eunuch (19:10). Jesus then responds to this counter argument that to be a eunuch for the Kingdom is a calling and not all people have this calling (19:11-12). Hence, to abstain from divorce should not imply abstinence from marriage.

In Mark 10:1-12, we find a similar argumentation structure to that of Matthew 19:1-12. The narrative of Mark begins with Jesus arriving at the region of Judea, with multitudes gathering around him as he began to teach them (10:1). The narrative then shifts to the test of the Pharisees *'Is it lawful for a man to divorce his wife?'* (10:2). Jesus then responds with a counter argument *'What did Moses command you?'* (10:3). The argument shifts to the Pharisees, reply that Moses permitted a man to write a certificate of divorce and dismiss his wife (10:4). The argument then shifts to the response of Jesus substantiating Moses' actions due to the *'hardness of their hearts'* and begins the creative narrative of God's original divine plan for mankind (10:5-9). The argument then changes to a new setting where his disciples ask him about the matter (10:10). This is followed by a reply from Jesus with reference to a man and woman committing adultery if they divorce with the intention to re-marry (10:11-12).

In Luke 16:14-18, we find a different argumentation structure. The narrative begins with the Pharisees *'deriding'* Jesus (16:14) proceeding a teaching to his disciples of those who faithfully use the wealth of this world for God's Kingdom, will be sufficiently trusted to receive the true riches of the Kingdom (16:1-13).

The argument then shifts to Jesus' response to the deriding of the Pharisees by stating that they should not justify themselves before men, because God knows their hearts (16:15). The argument then shifts to the Law. Jesus argued that although the period, which witnessed the formation of the Law and the prophets ceased when John the Baptist came, they did not become invalid. Rather, the smallest detail of the Law (*i.e.* *'tittle')* finds fulfilment in Jesus' preaching of the Kingdom of God. Jesus then argues that the Pharisees are without excuse (16:16-17). The argument then shifts to an example given by Jesus that if a man or woman divorce with the intention of re-marriage they commit adultery (16:18).

Classification of Argument

The next step in this exegetical process is to assess the greater rhetorical intention of the divorce discourse. In this section, we will focus on an identification of the genre of the texts of the Synoptic Gospels used in this research.

Narrative Analysis

In order to account adequately for the discourse nature of Matthew 19:1-12/ Mark10:1-12/Luke 16:18, it has to be situated and interpreted in terms of its function in the Matthew/Mark/Luke narratives as a whole. This point introduces us to the next stage in the theory and methodology, namely to account for the narrative nature of the Gospels.

Brown identifies the discourse between Jesus and the Pharisees as lively and direct storyteller's style (*i.e.* narratives).[79] Using Rimmon-Kenan's analysis, we will now discuss the following aspects, namely *(a) Narrative Theory as Story, (b) Narrative Theory as Text,* and *(c) Narrative Theory as Narration* (used in the analysis of Ezra and Nehemiah). Story comprises the logical chronological fictional events, which provide the narratives with the 'raw materials' in terms of which the narratives are told. The text comprises the narrative texts, which we read. Narration is the category that accounts for the process of the narrative production, - *i.e.* the existence of narrative implies that someone has written the narrative and has intended it to be read as message by a reader or readers.

In the following section I will analyze the concepts of *story, text and narration.*

Narrative Theory as Story

Following Bremond, an account of the divorce discourse between Jesus and the Pharisees has to take the nature of the *events and the characters* into consideration.[80]

Events in the Story

In the macro-narratives of Matthew/Mark/Luke, the function of events can be explicated through the potentiality of the narrative (objective defined: divorce) and its progression with the result of the objective reached (Is it lawful for a man to divorce his wife?). The function of Matthew 19:1-12/ Mark 10:1-12/Luke 16:18 within the logical chronological development (Kingdom ethics versus secular ethics), can be accounted for in terms of its relationship with earlier (analeptic) and later (proleptic) events in the story.

In Matthew 19:1-12, we find that the writer uses one event to relate the narrative. The confrontation with the Pharisees and the dialogue with the disciples all occur as Jesus had departed from Galilee and arrived at the region of Judea beyond Jordan, with great multitudes following him.

In Mark, however, we have two events. Mark 10:1-9 is the first event, which recants the discourse between Jesus and the Pharisees in the course of his journey (*i.e.* a public teaching). The second event is the dialogue between Jesus and the Disciples, which take place in another setting - *i.e.* a house (Mark 10:10-12 a private teaching). In Luke 16:18, the narrative has one event, the confrontation between Jesus and the Pharisees with an analeptic relation to a parable of the wise use of money (16:1-13) and a proleptic foreshadowing of the Richman and Lazarus (16:19-31).

Characters in the Story

For a distinction of characters on story level, we have made a distinction in the previous chapter and chapter one between flat and round characters. Flat characters have only one trait, quality or idea attached to them. Round characters are more complex and involves, having more than one quality and developing in the course of action.

Characters	**Matthew**	**Mark**	**Luke**
Jesus	19:1 Round	19:5 Round	16:14 Round
Moses	19:7 Flat	19:3-4 Flat	
Pharisees	19:3 Round	10:2 Round	16:14 Round
Disciples	19:10 Round	10:10 Round	16:1
Great Multitudes	19:2 Flat	10:1 Flat	
Eunuchs	19:12 Flat		

The Pharisees and the disciples are round characters with a few qualities attached to them. Jesus is complex to a greater degree in so far as he has many characteristics, labels and qualities attached to him during the course of the action in the story (*i.e.* teacher, healer etc.).

Narrative Theory as Text

Whereas the story only has a relation with the text, the text stands in relation to both story and narration. In order to account for the narrative text a distinction is made between the categories of *time, characterization* and *focalization.*

Time

The study of time concerns the textual arrangements of the event component of the story in the text. In the text, the narrative does not correspond to the logical chronological succession of events in the story. On the contrary, it sometimes deviates from it. Even though time in the narrative text as we read through it is inescapably linear, a comparison between text-time and story-time reveals that a hypothetical norm of complete correspondence between the two is only rarely realized. The discordances that these deviations in the text create can be studied through comparing the *order of events, duration of events* and *frequency of events.*

Order of Events

Order specifies the analeptic and proleptic relations between the length of time and event takes in the story and text time. In Matthew 19:1-12, examples can be found in the analeptic reference by Jesus to the divine plan of God for the institution of marriage (19:4-6) and in the foreshadowing of the Pharisees opposition to his teachings with the counter argument in 19:8-9. This is also evident in Mark 10:5-9.

In Matthew, the order of events follows a sequence of challenge by the Pharisees (19:3), a response by Jesus (19:4-6), a counter argument of the Pharisees (19:7) and a counter response by Jesus (19: 8-9), followed by a dialogue between Jesus and the disciples in 19:10-12.

A similar order of events is followed in Mark 10:1-12. In Mark 10:2, the Pharisees challenge Jesus. In Mark 10:5-9 Jesus responds to the challenge. However, there is no counter argument presented by the Pharisees in Mark's Narrative.

In Luke 16, the order of events differs. Jesus teaches a parable to the disciples. The Pharisees gathered to hear the teachings of Jesus and laughed at him. He then challenged the Pharisees on their interpretation of the Law, with special reference to their understanding of divorce, which they were currently debating.

Duration of Events

Duration specifies the difference between; the length of time an event takes in the story and textual levels. The reading of Jesus' discourse in Matthew 19:1-12 and Luke 16 basically takes the same time as what it has on the story level. However, in Mark we have a different scenario. The public teaching takes place in the course of Jesus' journey to Judea; however, the private teaching of the disciples (Mark 10:10-12) takes place in a new setting of a house. There is a lapse of time before Jesus' private teaching with his Disciples.

Frequency of Events

Frequency of events specifies the number of times an event is recounted in the text. This was a common literature style/feature of the ancient writers. However, in the texts exegeted in this chapter, all the events are singulative - *i.e.* related only once. Even though there are similarities in the signs of Jesus, his sayings, the responses of the crowds and his opposition, all these have a singulative character in this rhetorical unit.

Characterization

Characterization concerns the representation in the text of the character component of the story. We have two types of characterization prevalent in the synoptic texts exegeted above. The first being direct characterization and the second being indirect characterization. In Luke 16:14, we have a direct characterization of the Pharisees *'lovers of money'*. Through an indirect characterization *'deriding Jesus'* (Luke 16:14/Matthew 19:3/Mark10:2) we know that they opposed Jesus and his teachings. Through the direct characterization of the Pharisees by Jesus (16:15), we know that they justified themselves before men as righteous, upright holy people, but in the eyes of God they were seen as a sect of abomination.

Through indirect representation in Matthew 19:1-2 and Mark 10:1, we know that Jesus associated with the poor and those that needed his help. People followed him *'multitudes'*, those that probably needed the help of Jesus were the peasants. This is why the Pharisees attested Jesus, because he associated with the lower social class.

An important addition to the process of characterization in the narrative is the use of analogy in the names of characters. In Matthew/Mark/Luke, the characterization of Jesus takes place primarily through his action (Matt. 19:1-2 healing, Mk 10:1 teaching) and speech.

Focalization

Focalization is the angle of vision through which the story is filtered in the text, and verbally formulated by the narrator. The subject (the focalizer) is the agent whose perception orients the presentation, whereas the object (the focalized) is what the focalizer perceives. In analyzing focalization we will refer to three categories namely, *(a) The Perceptual facet, (b) The Psychological facet,* and *(c) The Ideological facet.*

The Perceptual facet

The perceptual facet (sight and hearing) is determined by time and space. In terms of time and space, the focalizers in Matthew 19:1-2/Mark 10:1-12/Luke 16:18 are all internal and not external to the action and interaction. Except for the narrator's commentaries (which is panchronic and which provides a bird's-eye view of the responses of the characters to Jesus), the focalizers do not provide a bird's-eye view of the action but participate in the action and are limited to the present character.[81] The focalized object in these narratives is the issue surrounding divorce *'Is it lawful for a man to divorce his wife'*.

The Psychological Facet

The psychological facet of perception has a cognitive and emotive component. The cognitive component (*i.e.* knowledge, conjecture, belief, memory) of the external narrator-focalizer is such that he knows everything about the represented world and about the character of

Jesus. He knows about the opposition of the Pharisees towards the teaching of Jesus. He is aware of the debate concerning the two interpretations of Deuteronomy 24:1 (Rabbi Shammai and Rabbi Hillel). He is also aware that Jesus' response to the challenge would support either one of the interpretations and clear the controversy. The characters in the narrative are limited to this knowledge. They all function as internal focalizers with limited knowledge. The emotive component comprises the emotions of the internal focalizers. In Luke 16:14 we find a clear expression of emotions - *i.e. 'derided Jesus', 'you are those who justify yourself before men'*. Here we find evident in Luke's writing that there was great animosity between Jesus and the Pharisees.

The Ideological Facet

The ideological facet of focalization comprises the norms of the text, which consist of a general system of viewing the world conceptually. In the narrative text, we find two ideologies prevalent.

The Ethical Ideology of the Pharisees (Secular Ethics): The first ideology is that of the Pharisees. Following the interpretation of Deuteronomy 24:1, the Pharisees perceived that Moses consented them the authority to divorce their wives provided that they issue them a certificate of divorce. The normal Jewish view according to rabbinic law was that a man could commit adultery against another married man, and a wife could be held to commit adultery against her husband, but a husband could not be held to commit adultery against his wife.

The Ethical Ideology of Jesus (Kingdom Ethics): The ideology of Jesus was contrary to that of the Pharisees. Jesus stated that the only reason Moses consented a divorce was due to the 'hardness of their hearts'. However, the initial will of God was for one man and one woman to join together in a bond in which they become one flesh. His ideology was substantiated by the original and divine plan of God for mankind. Secondly, Jesus emphasized (Mark 10:11) that a man could also commit adultery against his wife. In his ideology, he elevated the status of a woman to that of a man with regards to ethical accountability of adultery.

There is a clear clash of the ethical ideologies between Jesus (Kingdom ethics) and the Pharisees (Secular ethics). In the narrative texts of Matthew/Mark/Luke, the narrator-focalizer's norms or ideologies provide the single dominant perspective, which is taken as authoritative, and all other ideologies in the text (*i.e.* the ideology of the Pharisees) are evaluated from this higher position.[82] The ideology of Jesus is positively evaluated by the narrator-focalizer and is the same as his own. The ideology is communicated to the narratee as the ideology, which the narratee must hold too.

The focalization through the opposition focalizers – (The Pharisees) – provide a conflicting ideological perspective to the ethics of divorce. Since this ideological perspective, is evaluated negatively by the narrator-focalizer, this ethical ideology is to be rejected by the narratee.

Narrative Theory as Narration

Narration is that analytic category in narrative theory, which accounts for the act of narrating or telling the story. Minimally, the narrator can be defined as the agent who narrates or engages in some activities serving the needs of the narration. The needs of the narration as they pertain to Matthew 19:1-12/Mark 10:1-12/Luke 16:18, are primarily determined by the narrator's perceptions of time and space, the level of narration, the narrator's commentary, the narrator's cognition of objects and characters, and the narrator's ideological norms and values as well as speech representation. In Matthew/Mark/Luke, time is determined by 'ulterior narration'. The narrative events are narrated after they happened. The level of narration of Matthew 19:1-12, Mark 10:1-12 and Luke 16:18 are extra-diegetic. The narrator's commentary provides narrational explanations and commentary on the speech and action in the narratives. In Matthew 19:1-2 and Mark 10:1 the narrator's commentary sets the scene for the discourse. The narrator's commentary also provides us with the indirect characterization of the Pharisees (*i.e.* Matt. 19:3 *'testing him'* Luke 16:14 *'Pharisees who were lovers of money'*).

The narrator's cognition of objects and characters (animosity towards the Pharisees) comprise the cognitive elements, which the narrator holds. The narrator's knowledge about Jesus and His opponents is conveyed through the narrative to the narratee. The narrative structure (argument direction) and impact on the narratee is such that it wants to persuade the narratee to accept this knowledge too. The narrator's ideological norms and values are also to be shared by the narratee. This is closely related to the above point. Even though these elements of narration can be studied in terms of narrative focalization as they are revealed in the text, they must also be objectified and analyzed as part of the discourse of the narrator, *i.e.* as elements which form part of the interpretive community which the narrator represents (*e.g.* Adultery and illicit offspring and the significance of genealogical lineage). Such an objectification provides the interpreter with the contents of the symbolic world and the practices used by the narrator and members of this symbolic world. The speech representation in Matthew 19:1-12, Mark 10:1-12 and Luke 16:18 is mimesis. The narrator creates the allusion that it is not he who speaks. He is only showing the action.

CONTEXTUAL MEANING: HISTORICAL RE-CONSTRUCTION – MATTHEW 19:1-12/MARK 10:1-12/ LUKE 16:18 FROM A PERSPECTIVE OF AFRICA[83]

The institution of family in African society, as in most societies of the world, is founded on marriage. Similar to the definition of marriage given by Jesus in Matthew 19:4-6 and Mark 10:5-9, Hastings defined marriage in African society as 'the union, permanent at least by intention, of a man and woman for the purpose of procreation and the rearing of children and mutual assistance'.[84]

In considering that the above definition suggests a monogamous Western form of marriage, marriage could be redefined as 'the approved social pattern whereby two or more persons establish a family'.[85] In the traditional African society, marriage was not merely for the sake of procreation, it also included the elements of companionship and mutual assistance between men and women. However, in traditional African society, stress was laid upon the procreation and continuation of life as the dominant reason for marriage. This was similar to the situation in the Matthew, Mark and Luke where the continuation of the family lineage was an important element of marriage and genealogical lineage was of great significance.

Mbiti noted that marriage and procreation in African communities are a unity; without procreation, marriage is incomplete.[86] However, the institution of marriage had a wider and perhaps more central importance in the African societies. According to Kenyatta, 'Marriage is one of the most powerful means of maintaining the cohesion of society and of enforcing that conformity to the kinship system and to tribal organizations without which social life is impossible'.[87] Similar to the traditions of Ancient Israel and the society of Matthew, Mark and Luke, marriage in traditional African societies was a process comprising the important steps of courtship and betrothal, socially approved agreements and finally the ceremonies and the establishment of a conjugal relationship with rights and obligations. Parallel to the institution of marriage that prevailed in the communities of Matthew, Mark and Luke, marriage in the African societies involved the parents. Relationships initiated by parents were also common.

Marriage in the African traditional society also followed a system close to that of the *Mohar* where gifts are exchanged from the side of the man to that of the girl. This custom is called *bride price* or *bride-wealth.* In patrilineal African societies, bride-wealth played a dominant role and seemed to be regarded as a compensation for the loss of a family member. Bride-wealth was, therefore, considered an essential element in sealing the contract of a marriage.[88] Marriage was in general considered to be a life-long union, but could with adequate justification, be dissolved, similar to Matthew 19:1-12, Mark 10:1-12. Hastings observed that divorce was more difficult in the patrilineal African societies where bride-wealth was usually high and greatly valued, and much easier in the matrilineal societies where women had the greater authority in determining the nature of the marriage, the protection of the children and quite often the locality of the marrying couple.[89]

The major grounds justifying divorce included cruelty, charges of sorcery, incompatibility, quarrelling between co-wives, laziness, adultery, and in some cases, childlessness.[90] Adultery was also used as an exception clause for the grounds of divorce in the texts of Matthew 19:9. In the situation of bareness, the taking of another wife was the more common consequence than divorce. In a few African societies, divorce was so easy that a husband could simply send away the wife, similar to the society of the Pharisees where the liberal school of Rabbi Hillel taught that a man could divorce his wife for any reason that displeased him (Matt. 19:3). However, in majority of African societies, divorce went through a vigorous scrutiny of elders and was not approved easily.

Customs no matter how greatly valued by a particular society, are bound to be violated. That is why it was not uncommon in traditional African society to hear of forms of punishment meted against violators of such customs, including violation of the institution of marriages. There were cases of men stealing each other's wives, adultery and sexual violations resulting in illegitimate pregnancies and births.[91]

In the traditional African society, the deviations listed above, were handled by the community, with the intention of punishing the culprit and also purifying and sanctifying the community.[92] Remedial steps taken against the offenders were often retributive or aimed at compensating the aggrieved party rather than merely punishing the offender. Similar to the society of the New Testament, offences such as adultery evoked shame on those caught or found out in error rather than in guilt. According to Waruta, the African society was definitely not free of violators of the accepted social norms, including those pertaining to marriage. However, the society employed humane corrective measures where necessary.[93] Parallel to the situation of the *New Testament*, marriage in traditional African society was a community affair involving families and clans of the marrying couple. If a wife or husband was found violating the institution of marriage it brought shame to the clan and family. Hence, it would result in feuding of the families and clans to maintain the integrity of either the wife or husband.[94]

The phenomenon of the traditional African perspective of marriage, divorce and adultery illustrates striking parallels to the society of Matthew, Mark and Luke. Similar to the situation of the Synoptic Gospels, the question that emerges from an African perspective is: *'Is it lawful for a man to divorce his wife?'* In considering a historical re-construction, both the society of the *New Testament* and the African society, stressed the importance of a proper institution of marriage. However, as noted by Waruta, 'customs no matter how greatly valued by society, were bound to be violated.'[95]

CONCLUSION

In considering Gottwald's definition that the society depicted in the

Bible is a real historical society, the Synoptic Gospels illustrate the problems endured by a real historical society of the institutions of marriage and divorce.[96] After analyzing the texts of the New Testament, we find a contradiction to the deduction of the analysis in the Old Testament. In Ezra and Nehemiah, the institution of divorce was compelled upon particular members of the community to rectify their social disparagement. However, the same institution that was compelled upon the members of society, was prohibited in the New Testament.

In a confrontation between Jesus and the Pharisees in Matthew 19:1-12, Mark 10:1-12 and Luke 16:18, the Pharisees questioned Jesus: *'Is it lawful for a man to divorce his wife?'* Jesus replied to the question by stating the original divine purpose of humanity, which implied the joining of *one man* and *one woman* (monogamous relationship) to form *one flesh.* It would seem as though Jesus didn't answer the question of the Pharisees, but instead emphasized the divine institution of marriage. However, according to Matthew 19:9, divorce was acceptable in the case of adultery.

In a society where divorce was an acceptable social norm, the institution of divorce was abused to meet the personal needs of individuals. In Mark 10:11-12, Jesus condemned divorce with the intention to re-marry as committing an offence of adultery. The question that is posed to Jesus, *'Is it lawful for a man to divorce his wife?'* - was a current debated topic amongst the Pharisees. They accepted that Moses consented divorce on the grounds that they issued the wife with a certificate of divorce, however, the rabbinical schools of interpretation differed on the meaning of the clause *'uncleanness in her'* (Deuteronomy 24:1). As a result they differed on the grounds for divorce.

After analyzing the Old Testament and New Testament Texts, we will now analyze the Jewish procedure of divorce and the Agunah problem in the next chapter.

NOTES

1. Malina JB, *The New Testament World*, John Knox Press, Atlanta, 1981, p. 23.
2. Ibid. p. 24.
3. Austin JL, *How to Do Things with Words*, Harvard University Press, Cambridge, 1962, p. 100.

4. Malina JB, *The New Testament World*, John Knox Press, Atlanta, 1981, p. 110.
5. Ibid. p. 110.
6. Ibid. p. 110.
7. Ibid. p. 110.
8. Ibid. p. 111.
9. Davies SL, *The New Testament: A Contemporary Introduction*, Harper and Row, San Francisco, 1988, p. 19.
10. Malina JB, *The New Testament World*, John Knox Press, Atlanta, 1981, p. 111.
11. Ibid. p. 112.
12. Ibid. p. 112.
13. Ibid. p. 112.
14. Ibid. p. 112.
15. Ibid. p. 112.
16. Kee HC, *The New Testament in Context: Sources and Documents*, Prentice-Hall, Englewood Cliffs, New Jersey, 1984, p. 183.
17. Ibid. p. 183.
18. Miller RJ, *The Complete Gospels*, Harper Collins, San Francisco, 1992, p. 56.
19. Ibid. p. 56.
20. Guthrie D, Motyer JA, *New Bible Commentary,* (3rd Edition), Inter-Varsity Press, Leicester, England, p. 814.
21. Ibid. p. 814.
22. Ibid. p. 814.
23. Ibid. p. 814.
24. Miller RJ, *The Complete Gospels*, Harper Collins, San Francisco, 1992, p. 10.
25. Ibid. p. 10.
26. Ibid. p. 10.
27. Ibid. p. 12.
28. Ibid. p. 114.
29. Ibid. p. 117.
30. Ibid. p. 117.
31. Ibid. p. 117.
32. Guthrie D, Motyer JA, *New Bible Commentary,* (3rd Edition), Inter-Varsity Press, Leicester, England, p. 840.
33. Hill D, *The Gospel of Matthew*, Marshall, Morgan and Scott, London, 1972, p. 278.
34. Filson VF, *The Gospel according to St. Matthew*, Adam and Charles Black, London, 1975, p. 205.
35. Guthrie D, Motyer JA, *New Bible Commentary,* (3rd Edition), Inter-Varsity Press, Leicester, England, p. 840.
36. Filson VF, *The Gospel according to St. Matthew*, Adam and Charles Black, London, 1975, p. 206.
37. Anderson H, *The Gospel of Mark*, Marshall, Morgan and Scott, London, 1976, p. 240.

38. Filson VF, *The Gospel according to St. Matthew*, Adam and Charles Black, London, 1975, p. 206.
39. Ibid. p. 206.
40. Ibid. p. 207.
41. Hill D, *The Gospel of Matthew*, Marshall, Morgan and Scott, London, 1972, p. 279.
42. Brown RE, *An Introduction to the New Testament*, Doubleday, New York, 1997, p. 194-195.
43. Hill D, *The Gospel of Matthew*, Marshall, Morgan and Scott, London, 1972, p. 279.
44. Ibid. p. 279.
45. Filson VF, *The Gospel according to St. Matthew*, Adam and Charles Black, London, 1975, p. 207.
46. Ibid. p. 207.
47. Hill D, *The Gospel of Matthew*, Marshall, Morgan and Scott, London, 1972, p. 281.
48. Guthrie D, Motyer JA, *New Bible Commentary,* (3rd Edition), Inter-Varsity Press, Leicester, England, p. 840.
49. Anderson H, *The Gospel of Mark*, Marshall, Morgan and Scott, London, 1976, p. 240.
50. Ibid. p. 241.
51. Ibid. p. 242.
52. Ibid. p. 242.
53. Ibid. p. 242.
54. Ibid. p. 243.
55. Guthrie D, Motyer JA, *New Bible Commentary,* (3rd Edition), Inter-Varsity Press, Leicester, England, p. 914.
56. Hill D, *The Gospel of Matthew*, Marshall, Morgan and Scott, London, 1972, p. 279.
57. Ibid. p. 280.
58. Ibid. p. 281.
59. Ibid. p. 282.
60. Anderson H, *The Gospel of Mark*, Marshall, Morgan and Scott, London, 1976, p. 243.
61. Ibid. p. 244.
62. Ibid. p. 244.
63. Ibid. p. 244.
64. Malina BJ & Rohrbaugh RL, *Social Science Commentary on the Synoptic Gospels*, Fortress Press, Minneapolis, 1992, pp. 120-122.
65. Ibid. p. 121.
66. Ibid. p. 121.
67. Ibid. p. 121.
68. Rewers E, *Language and Space: The Poststructuralist Turn in the Philosophy of Culture*, Peter Lang, Frankfurt am Main, 1999, pp. 128-130. A dialogue with the Disciples stands in contrast to the argumentative discourse between Jesus and the Pharisees.
69. Davies SL, *The New Testament: A Contemporary Introduction*, Harper and Row, San Francisco, 1988, p. 19.

70. Ibid. pp. 19-20.
71. Ibid. p. 19.
72. Ibid. p. 20.
73. Ibid. p. 19.
74. Guthrie D, Motyer JA, *New Bible Commentary,* (3rd Edition), Inter-Varsity Press, Leicester, England, p. 914.
75. Hester J, *Re-discovering and Re-inventing Rhetoric, Scriptura,* Journal of the Bible and Theology in Southern Africa, Vol. No. 50, July 1994, p.4.
76. Ibid. p. 5.
77. Perelman C and Olbrechts-Tyteca L, *The New Rhetoric: A Treatise on Argumentation,* University Press of Notre Dame, Notre Dame, 1971, p. 51.
78. Hester J, *Re-discovering and Re-inventing Rhetoric, Scriptura,* Journal of the Bible and Theology in Southern Africa, Vol. No. 50, July 1994, p. 6.
79. Brown RE, *An Introduction to the New Testament,* Doubleday, New York, 1997, pp. 194-195.
80. Bremond C, *De logika van de narrative mogelijkheden.* In Fokkema DM & Ibsch E (eds), *Teksboek algemene literatuurwetenschap: moderne ontwikkelingen in de literatuurwetenschap geïllustreerd in een bloemlesing uit Nederlandse en buitelandse publikaties,* Ambo, Baarn, 1977.
81. Rimmon-Kenan S, *Narrative Fiction: Contemporary Poetics,* Methuen, London, 1983, p. 78.
82. Ibid. p. 81.
83. In developing a contextual meaning - *i.e.* historical reconstruction, I hosted four workshops. These workshops were held on the 6th / 13th/ 20th/ 27th September 2001 at Bluff Christian Church (Assemblies of God-SA) situated at 240 Bluff Road, Jacobs, Kwa-Zulu Natal, South Africa. In these workshops, I invited members from the local informal settlements and the squatter camps to participate in an academic research (an attendance of +/- 50 people per workshop). The intention of these workshops was to involve ordinary readers from disadvantaged communities to share their knowledge and insight on Biblical interpretation and African marriage customs. The information I obtained from these workshops has helped me to develop the following contextual meaning and historical reconstruction of Matthew 19:1-12, Mark 10:1-12 and Luke 16: 18.
84. Hastings A, *Christian Marriage in Africa,* SPCK, London, 1973, p. 27.
85. Horton PB & Chester LH, *Sociology,* (2nd Ed.), McGraw-Hill Book Company, New York, 1968, p. 216.
86. Mbiti JS, *African Religions and Philosophy,* Heinemann, London, 1969, pp. 225-228.
87. Kenyatta J, *Facing Mount Kenya,* Secker & Warburg, London, 1938, p. 64.
88. Waruta DW, *Marriage and Family in Contemporary African Society,* in Warutu DW & Kinoti HW, *Pastoral Care in African Christianity,* Action Publishers, Nairobi 2000, p. 104.
89. Hastings A, *Christian Marriage in Africa,* SPCK, London, 1973, p. 35.
90. Waruta DW, *Marriage and Family in Contemporary African Society,* in Warutu DW & Kinoti HW, *Pastoral Care in African Christianity,* Action Publishers, Nairobi 2000, p. 105.

91. Ibid. p. 106.
92. Ibid. p. 106.
93. Ibid. p. 107.
94. Ibid. pp. 106-107.
95. Ibid. p. 106.
96. Gottwald NK, *The Tribes of Yahweh: The Sociology of the Religion of the Liberated Israel*, Orbis Books, Maryknoll, New York, 1979.

5

THE JEWISH PROVISION FOR DIVORCE AND THE AGUNAH PROBLEM

INTRODUCTION

Divorce as a Jewish institution had its origin in pre-Israelite times. The Torah (Deuteronomy 24:1) gives the details of the procedure when a man puts away his wife; but these are given only incidentally in connection with another law forbidding the husband to re-marry his divorced wife, if in the meantime, she had been the wife of another man. As noted in the previous chapters, an understanding of the Jewish provision and prohibition of divorce is essential for the understanding of the *Old Testament* and *New Testament* texts. Hence, in this chapter, I will briefly analyze the Jewish provision and prohibition for divorce, the procedure of divorce and the *Agunah* problem.

THE JEWISH PROVISION AND PROHIBITION OF DIVORCE

According to Deuteronomy 22: 19-29, if a man falsely impugned his wife's chastity he was punished by not being allowed to divorce her. If he seduced a virgin, he had to marry her and could never divorce her. These passages clearly show that as far as the Biblical legislation is concerned, the husband's right to divorce his wife was unquestioned. However, the wife had no right to ask for a divorce, and her consent was not required in case the husband wished to divorce her. According to Landman, the Israelites merely followed the customs, which were common to the people of the East.[1] However, with the growing moral sense of the Jewish people, and with the greater realization of the sanctity of marriage and the necessity of maintaining the integrity of the family, an effort became apparent to diminish the frequency of divorce and to protect the wife against hardships to which it subjected her.

One of the methods of combating divorce was by appealing to the affections and moral sense of the husband. The prophet Malachi (Mal. 2:13-16) upbraids those who divorce the *'wife of their youth'*. The Talmud expanded this passage and stated that 'if anyone divorces the partner of his youth, the altar sheds tears on his account' and 'whosoever, divorces his wife is hateful in the sight of God' (Git. 90ab).

Legislation further sought to limit the husband's right to divorce his wife at will.[2] The *Mishnah* forbade him to do so in case his wife was insane (Yeb. 14:1), in captivity (Keth. 4:9) or if she was a very young minor. There was considerable discussion as to the permissible grounds for divorce, depending on the interpretation of Deut. 24:1- *'because he had found some unseemly thing in her'*. The older view represented by the school of Shammai, held that only unchastity on the part of the wife could justify a divorce.[3] However, this extreme view seems to have brought about a reaction in Jewish thought, for the later view tended to extend the grounds for divorce. The more liberal school of Rabbi Hillel interpreted the Biblical expressions to mean any reason whatsoever and gives as an example: *'even if she spoils a dish in cooking'*.[4] This view has prevailed in Judaism and grounds for divorce are not required for a voluntary dissolution of marriage.

However, the rabbis had found more effective means of combating the evils of divorce. Thus, it was required that if a husband divorces his wife, he must return to her all the property which she had brought into the marriage, as well as any other sum he may have assigned her as her marriage portion.[5] Another provision required that a divorce must take place in the presence of a court of rabbis, thus affording the opportunity for reconciliation and safeguarding of the wife's interest.[6] Finally, Rabbi Gershom secured the passage of a resolution requiring the consent of the wife before the husband was permitted to divorce her.[7] However, there are certain grounds on which the authorities could compel a divorce. In Jewish law, the following are generally allowed as grounds for divorce on the part of the husband. (1) Suspicion of adultery; (2) breach of moral deportment on the part of the wife;

(3) the wife's refusal to have marital intercourse; (4) refusal to move the husband's place of domicile; (5) violations of religious ordinances in the wife's management of the household.[8] The following are the grounds on which a wife can demand a divorce from her husband : (1) The husband's following a disgraceful vocation; (2) cruelty to the wife; (3) refusing to provide.[9] The wife herself could not divorce her husband, but upon her appeal, the court would endeavor to compel him to divorce her, usually by threatening him with ex-communication and sometimes by appeal to non-Jewish courts.

In the following cases, the courts could compel a divorce without the consent of the parties namely, adultery of the wife, or justifiable suspicion of adulterous behaviour; if the marriage contract was contrary to Jewish law; the leprosy of one of the couples; if the marriage remains childless after ten years (Yeb. 64a).

DIVORCE PROCEEDINGS

A marriage consecrated according to the Law of Moses and Israel is not dissolved except through the Law of Moses and Israel.[10] Its procedure, based upon Biblical precept, is strictly governed by the *halakha*. According to Rabbi Donin, divorces granted under Secular or Civil Law by civil authorities have no validity under Jewish Law.[11] Civil divorces possess no moral or spiritual significance in severing the consecrated bonds of religious marriage. Rabbi Donin substantiated that, the divorce proceedings must be supervised by a Beth Din (a rabbinic court consisting of three rabbis competent in the laws of marriage and divorce).[12] In addition to the Beth Din, a scribe (*sofer*) and two witnesses comprise the personnel needed in the issuance of a Jewish divorce (*get*). Only after effort is made to reconcile the couple, the grounds for a divorce are sufficiently compelling, and mutually agreed property settlement has been reached, will a Beth Din issue a divorce.

The entire procedure may take one and a half to two hours.[13] The bulk of time is taken up by the writing of the *get* by the scribe. The document is lettered like and is similar in appearance to a column of a Torah Scroll. The *get* is written individually on behalf of the husband and the wife. It contains their names, the date, and the name of the city where it was written. However, the document itself mentions no grounds for divorce and no charge by either husband or wife.

The following is a translation of an Ashkenazi *get*, according to the general usage in the Diaspora:[14]

On the.................day of the week, the.....................day of the month of.................................

In the year...... from the creation of the world according to the calendar reckoning we are accustomed to count here, in the city......(which is also known as......), which is located on the river..........(and on the river.........) and situated near wells of water, I,....... (also known as.........), the son of..........(also known as...........), who today am present in the city..........(also known as...........), which is located on the river..........(and on the river.........) and situated near wells of water, do willingly consent, being under no restraint, to release, to set free, and put aside thee, my wife.......(also known as..........), the daughter of...................(also known as................), who art in the city of ....(also known as............), which is located on the river..........(and on the river.........) and situated near wells of water, who has been my wife from before. Thus do I set free, release thee, and put thee aside, in order that thou may have permission and the authority over thyself to go and marry any man that thou may desire. No person may hinder thee from this day onward, and thou art permitted to every man. This shall be for thee from me a bill of dismissal, a letter of release, and a document of freedom, in accordance with the laws of Moses and Israel.

.............the son of............witness
.............the son of............witness

Following the writing of the *get*, both husband and wife are asked a number of routine questions to ascertain their free will and consent in the divorce action. While the formal ceremony, based upon Biblical verses, provides for the husband to give the *get* and for the wife to receive it, this is basically procedural. In actual practice, one does not give nor does the other receive without the actual consent and approval of each. This is especially so in countries outside of Israel, where Jewish religious courts do not possess the power to compel a husband to consent to give the *get*, or compel a wife to consent to receive the *get*.[15] Only moral pressure can be exercised in these situations.

The bill of divorce cannot be printed. They must be written in entirety, specifically for the particular man and the particular woman for the specific purpose of effecting, the particular divorce. The proceedings are simplest when both the husband and the wife are present at the same time. However, should this be difficult or undesirable for them to meet, it is possible to arrange for the proceedings to be finalized through the appointment of a messenger. In this case, the husband places the document into the hands of the messenger who acts on behalf of the husband. One member of the Beth Din, one of the witnesses, or the scribe himself may serve as the messenger.[16]

After the proceedings are completed, a tear is made in the divorce document to indicate that it has been used and cannot be used again. The document itself is retained by the Beth Din and kept in a permanent file. Official letters, called a release (*ptur*) are given to the man and woman testifying that the *get* has taken place and affirming their right to re-marry. The woman may not remarry following the *get* for a period of ninety-two days.[17] The reason for the waiting period is to remove all doubts as to paternity which might be raised should she marry and conceive right away.

The laws relating to the writing of a document valid according to *halakha* and to the proceedings themselves are numerous and complex. None but the most learned in the law of divorce may preside over it, lest an error result in the invalidation of the *get*.

THE *AGUNAH* PROBLEM

The problem of the *agunah*: a woman, whose husband has disappeared or is otherwise unable to terminate the marriage by executing a bill of divorce, has long been the source of much hardships and heartache. Also the consequences of war, has the disastrous side effects of increasing the *agunot*. Since *Halakha* does not sanction re-marriage in the absence of positive proof of death, the wife of a soldier (presumed dead) becomes bereft of her husband yet forbidden to re-marry.[18] The tragic plight of the *agunah* has spurred rabbinic authorities throughout the generations to seek possible means of remedying such grievous situations. The earliest attempt to mitigate the *agunah* problem, date to Biblical times. The Gemara, Ketubot 9b, states that the participants in the wars of King David, delivered bills of divorce to their wives before leaving for battle. According to Rashi, such divorces were conditional becoming effective in the event of the husband's failure to return.[19] The Gemara, Shabbat 56a, cites this practice in explanation of the dictum, *'one who claims that David was a sinner is mistaken'*. Bat-Sheva, according to the Talmud, was no longer the wife of Uriah. Since, Uriah had followed the usual procedure and presented his wife with a bill of divorce before undertaking his military assignment.[20] According to Ba'al ha-Turim, this practice was not an innovation of King David, but was originally introduced by Moses prior to the military engagements leading to the conquest of the land of Canaan.[21] However, the purpose of the practice as instituted by Moses was somewhat more limited and was employed merely to obviate the necessity for the Levirate marriage.

Throughout the years conditional divorces were at times granted in order to obviate other causes of the *agunah* situation. The widespread controversy surrounding the famed *'Divorce of Vienna'* centers around the above problem.[22] A young man sixteen years of age became afflicted with a severe illness and agreed to present his wife with a bill of divorce. At the time of the divorce proceedings, the husband's consent was obtained by convincing him that the divorce was being executed solely for the purpose of exempting his young wife from *halizah* (the ceremony for the release of a widow). However, upon his recovery, his wife would return to him. The young man was restored to health, but his wife refused to resume the marital relationship. The matter was brought before the renowned Maharam of Lublin, who ruled that in the light of this understanding, the husband's recovery invalidated the original divorce.[23]

R. Mordecai Jaffe forbade the woman to re-marry. In the light of Deuteronomy 24:1-2, he stated that the woman may become the *'wife of another man'* only if she has been divorced by her husband because *'she does not find favour in his eyes'*.[24] A bill of divorce whose presentation is not motivated by a loss of *'favour'* is not effective as an instrument empowering marriage to another.

CONCLUSION

In conclusion we note that the realities of life continue. Unfortunately,

Israel is enveloped in a seemingly endless state of warfare, and the *agunah* problem is both real and heart rendering. Under these circumstances, every possible measure should be taken to prevent any such unfortunate occurrence. The formula adopted in the past where a soldier issued his wife with a conditional bill of divorce, which would become effective if he did not return, generates feelings of distaste and hesitation. In reality, it represents an emergency measure expressing the acme of forethought, concern and devotion. Any precaution is clearly worthwhile if only to avoid a single case of anguish and tragedy.[25]

NOTES

1. Landman I, *The Universal Jewish Encyclopedia*, (Volume 3), Universal Jewish Encyclopedia Press, New York, 1941, p. 577.
2. Ibid. p. 578.
3. Ibid. p. 578.
4. Ibid. p. 578.
5. Ibid. p. 578.
6. Ibid. p. 578.
7. Ibid. p. 578.
8. Lipkin J, *Encyclopedia Judaica*, (Vol. 6 Di-Fo), Keter Publishing House, Jerusalem, Israel, 1971, pp. 128-132.
9. Ibid. pp. 128-132.
10. Donin HH, *To be a Jew: A Guide to Jewish observance in Contemporary Life*, Basic Books, New York, 1972, p. 292.
11. Ibid. p. 292.
12. Ibid. p. 293.
13. Ibid. p. 293.
14. Lipkin J, *Encyclopedia Judaica*, (Vol. 6 Di-Fo), Keter Publishing House, Jerusalem, Israel, 1971, p.132.
15. Donin HH, *To be a Jew: A Guide to Jewish observance in Contemporary Life*, Basic Books, New York, 1972, p. 293.
16. Ibid. p. 293.
17. Ibid. p. 293.
18. Ibid. p. 293.
19. Bleich JD, *Contemporary Halakhic Problems*, Volume 1, KTAV Publishing House, New York, 1977, p. 151.
20. Ibid. p. 152.
21. Ibid. p. 151.
22. Ibid. p. 153.
23. Ibid. p. 152.
24. Ibid. p. 152.
25. Ibid. p. 154.

Bibliography

Ackroyd PR, *1 and 2 Chronicles, Ezra and Nehemiah*, (Torch Bible Commentaries), SCM Press, London, 1973.

Ackroyd PR, *Chronicles-Ezra-Nehemiah: The Concept of Unity*, Zeitschrift für katholische Theologie, Supplement Series 100, 1988.

Alcalay R, *Words of the Wise: An Anthology of Proverbs and Practical Axioms*, Massada Press, Jerusalem, Israel, 1970.

Alexander P *(et al.), The Lion Concise Bible Encyclopedia*, Lion Publishing, England, 1980.

Alter R, *The Art of Biblical Narrative*, George Allen & Unwin, London, 1981.

Austin JL, *How to Do Things with Words*, Harvard University Press, Cambridge, 1962.

Barr J, *History and Ideology in the Old Testament: Biblical Studies at the end of a Millennium*, Oxford University Press, Oxford, 2000.

Batten L, *Ezra and Nehemiah*, T&T Clark, Edinburg, 1980.

Batten LW, *A Critical Exegetical Commentary on the Books of Ezra and Nehemiah*, T&T Clark, Edinburg, 1961.

Bleich JD, *Contemporary Halakhic Problems*, Volume 1, KTAV Publishing House, New York, 1977.

Blenkinsopp J, *Ezra-Nehemiah*, SCM Press, London, 1988.

Bowman RA, *Introduction and Exegesis to the Books of Ezra and Nehemiah*, (Interpreter's Bible Vol. 3), Abingdon Press, Nashville, New York, 1954.

Bremond C, *De logika van de narrative mogelijkheden.* In Fokkema DM & Ibsch E (eds), *Teksboek algemene literatuurwetenschap: moderne ontwikkelingen in de literatuurwetenschap geïllustreerd in een bloemlesing uit Nederlandse en buitelandse publikaties*, Ambo, Baarn, 1977.

Brockington LH, *Ezra, Nehemiah and Ester*, Thomas Nelson and Sons, England, 1969.

Brown RE, *An Introduction to the New Testament*, Doubleday, New York, 1997.

Bultmann R, *The History of the Synoptic Tradition*, Harper and Row, New York, 1963.

Camp C, *Wisdom and the Feminine in the Book of Proverbs*, Bible and Literature, Volume 11, Almond Press, Sheffield, 1985.

Childs BS, *'Introduction to Old Testament as Scripture'*, SCM Press Ltd., London 1979.

Christopher S, *The Mixed Marriage Crisis in Ezra*, in Eskenazi TC & Richards KH, *Second Temple Studies: 2 Temples and Community in the Persian period*, JSOT Press, Sheffield, England, 1994.

Clinebell H, *Basic Types of Pastoral Care and Counseling*, Abingdon Press, Nashville, Tennessee, 1984.

Clines DJA, *Ezra, Nehemiah and Ester*, (New Century Bible), Eerdmans, Grand Rapids, London, 1984.

Clines DJA, *Interested Parties: The ideology of Writers and Readers of the Hebrew Bible*, *Journal for the study of Old Testament,* Supplement Series 205, Gender, Culture, Theory 1, Sheffield Academic Press, England, 1995.

Coggins RJ, *The Books of Ezra and Nehemiah*, Cambridge University Press, Cambridge, 1976.

Culler J, *Literary Theory*, Oxford University Press, New York, 1997.

Davies RP, *In search of Ancient Israel*, *Journal for the Study of Old Testament,* Supplement Series 148, JSOT Press, Sheffield, 1992.

Davies SL, *The New Testament: A Contemporary Introduction*, Harper and Row, San Francisco, 1988.

Davies WD, Finkelstein L, *The Cambridge History of Judaism: The Persian Period*, Cambridge University Press, Cambridge, 1984.

Donin HH, *To be a Jew: A Guide to Jewish observance in Contemporary Life*, Basic Books, New York, 1972.

Douglas M, *In The Wilderness: The Doctrine of Defilement in the Book of Numbers*, Journal for the Study of Old Testament, Supplement Series 158, Sheffield Academic Press, England, 1993.

Eisenstadt SN, *Comments on the problem of continuity of Jewish historical patterns in Israeli society*, in Kahane R and Kopstein

S (eds), *Problems of collective identity and legitimation in the Israeli society: A Reader*, Academon, Jerusalem, 1980.

Emerton JA, *Nehemiah, Journal for Theological Studies,* Series 23, 1972.

Eric Partridge, *Origins: An Etymological Dictionary of Modern English*, Oxford Press, London, 1966.

Exum & Clines, *The New Literary Criticism and the Hebrew Bible, Journal for the Study of Old Testament (JSOT)*, Supplement series 143, Sheffield, England, 1993.

Ezkenazi TC & Judd PE, *Marriage to a Stranger in Ezra 9-10*, in Eskenazi TC & Richards KH, *Second Temple Studies: 2 Temples and Community in the Persian period*, JSOT Press, Sheffield, England, 1994.

Ezkenazi TC, Richard HK, *Second Temple Studies: 2 Temple and Community in the Persian Period*, Sheffield Academic Press, England, 1994.

Fensham FC, *The Books of Ezra and Nehemiah*, (The New International Commentary on the Old Testament), Eerdmans, Grand Rapids, 1982.

Filson VF, *The Gospel according to St. Matthew*, Adam and Charles Black, London, 1975.

Friedman M, *The Chief Rabbinate- Dilemma without solution*, in Kahane R and Kopstein S (eds), *Problems of collective identity and legitimation in the Israeli society: A Reader*, Academon, Jerusalem, 1980.

Genette G, *Narrative Discourse*, Blackwell, Oxford, 1972.

Gerrig RJ, *Experiencing Narrative World: On the Psychological Activities of Reading*, Yale University Press, New Haven, London, 1993.

Gottwald NK, *The Hebrew Bible: A Socio-Literary introduction*, Fortress Press, Philadelphia, 1985.

Gottwald NK, *The Tribes of Yahweh: A Sociology of the Religion of the Liberated Israel*, Orbis Books, Maryknoll, New York, 1979.

Gray J, *The Canaanites – Ancient Peoples and Places*, Thames and Hudson, London, 1964.

Guthrie D, Motyer JA, *New Bible Commentary,* (3rd Edition), Inter-Varsity Press, Leicester, England, 1970.

Hastings A, *Christian marriage in Africa*, SPCK, London, 1973.

Hester J, *Place the Blame: The presence of the Epideictic Galations One and Two*, unpublished manuscript, 1987.

Hester J, *Re-discovering and Re-inventing Rhetoric, Scriptura*, Journal of Bible and Theology in Southern Africa, Vol. 50, (July) 1994.

Hill D, *The Gospel of Matthew*, Marshall, Morgan and Scott, London, 1972.

Hoffmann RJ, *The Moral Rhetoric of the Gospels: Biblical* verses *Secular Ethics*, Prometheus, Buffalo, 1988.

Hoglund K, *Achaemenid Imperial Administration in Syria-Palestine and the Missions of Ezra and Nehemiah*, (PhD Dissertation) Duke University 1989 *published in* 1992.

Hoglund KG, *The Achaemenid Context*, in Davies PR, *Second Temple Studies*, Journal for the Study of Old Testament, Series 117, JSOT Press, Sheffield, 1991.

Horton PB & Chester LH, *Sociology*, (2nd Ed.), McGraw-Hill Book Company, New York, 1968.

Kapelrud AS, *The Question of Authorship in the Ezra Narrative: A Lexical Investigation*, Oslo, Dybwad, 1944.

Kee HC, *The New Testament in Context: Sources and Documents*, Prentice-Hall, Englewood Cliffs, New Jersey, 1984.

Kelber WH, *The Oral and Written Gospel: The Hermeneutics of Speaking and Writing in the Synoptic Tradition*, Fortress Press, Philadelphia, 1983.

Kennedy GA, *Classical and Christian Source Criticism: The Relationships among the Gospels: An Inter-disciplinary Dialogue*, Trinity University Press, San Antonio, 1978.

Kenyatta J, *Facing Mount Kenya*, Secker & Warburg, London, 1938.

Kidner FD, *Ezra and Nehemiah*, (Tyndale Old Testament Commentaries), Inter-Varsity Press, Leicester, 1979.

Landman I, *The Universal Jewish Encyclopedia*, (Volume 3), KTAV Publishing, New York, 1941.

Lichtman G, *Hashalom : Finding Solutions to the Aguna Dilemma*, (NS) Vol. 5. No. 5, 2001.

Lipkin J, *Encyclopedia Judaica*, (Vol. 6 Di-Fo), Keter Publishing House, Jerusalem, Israel, 1971.

Longenecker BW, *2 Esdras*, Sheffield Academic Press, Sheffield, England, 1995.

Malina JB & Rohrbaugh RL, *Social Science Commentary on the Synoptic Gospels*, Fortress Press, Minneapolis, 1992.

Malina JB, *The New Testament World*, John Knox Press, Atlanta, 1981.

Mbiti JS, *African Religions and Philosophy*, Heinemann, London, 1969.

Merton RK, *Inter-marriage and the Social Structure: Fact and Theory*, Issue 9 Psychiatry, 1941.

Milgrom J, *Numbers*, The JPS Torah Commentary, Jewish Publication Society, Philadelphia, 1990.

Miller RJ, *The Complete Gospels*, Harper Collins, San Francisco, 1992.

Muilenburg J, *Form Criticism and Beyond*, Journal of Biblical Literature, Vol. 88, 1969.

Myers JM, *Ezra, Nehemiah*, (Anchor Bible), Doubleday, Garden City, 1965.

Noth M, *The Chronicler's History*, Journal for the Study of Old Testament, Supplement Series 50, JSOT Press, Sheffield, 1987.

Perelman C and Olbrechts – Tyteca L, *The New Rhetoric: A Treatise on Argumentation*, University of Notre Dame Press, Notre Dame, 1971.

Pritchard JB, *Ancient Near Eastern Texts to the Old Testament*, (3rd edition), Princeton University Press, Princeton, 1969 (Translation to the Ancient Near Eastern Royal Inscriptions).

Pritchard JB, *The Ancient Near East: An Anthology of Texts and Pictures*, Princeton University Press, England, 1958.

Rahman SA, *Punishment of Apostasy in Islam*, Zarreen Art Press, Lahore, 1972.

Rewers E, *Language and Space: The Post-structuralist Turn in the Philosophy of Culture*, Peter Lang, Frankfurt am Main, 1999.

Rimmon Kenan S, *Narrative Fiction: Contemporary Poetics*, Methuen, London, 1983.

Roland de Vaux, *Ancient Israel- Its Life and Institutions*, Darton, Longman and Todd, London, 1965.

Rudolph W, *Esra-Nehemia*, P. Siebeck, HAT, Tübingen, 1949.

Ryle HE, *The Books of Ezra and Nehemiah*, (The Cambridge Bible for Schools and Colleges), Cambridge University Press, Cambridge, 1897.

Segre DV, *A Crisis of identity: Israel and Zionism*, Oxford University Press, Oxford, 1980.

Simpson JA, Weiner ESC, *The Oxford English Dictionary*, (2nd Edition), Vol. VI, Clarendon Press, Oxford, 1989.

Singer I, *The Jewish Encyclopedia*, (Volume 4) KTAV Publishing House, New York, (?)

Smit JA, *Discourse and power in the Gospel according to Mark : Strategies of Exclusion, Koers* - Bulletin for Christian Scholarship, Vol. 58 No. 1, 1993.

Smit JA, *Mark as interpretive Narrative*, SAVAL Conference, Papers XII, Potchefstroom, March 1993.

Smit JA, *The positive unconscious knowledge in Mark*, SAVAL Conference, Papers XI, Potchefstroom, April 1992.

Smith DL, *Religion and the Landless*, Meyer-Stone, Bloomington, 1989.

Smith M, *Palestine Parties and Politics that shaped the Old Testament*, Columbia University Press, New York, 1971.

Smith M, *Palestinian Parties and Politics that Shaped the Old Testament*, SCM Press, London, 1987.

Snijders LA, *The Meaning of ZERAH in the Old Testament*, Old Testament Studies, Volume 10, 1954.

Torrey CC, *The Composition and Historical Value of Ezra-Nehemiah*, Beihefte Zur Zaw, Giessen, Ricker, 1896.

Uspensky B, *A Poetics of Composition*, University of California Press, Berkeley, 1973.

Van der Toorn K, *Female Prostitution in Payment of Vows in Ancient Israel, Journal of Biblical Literature*, Volume 108, 1989.

Vinson RB, *A Comparative Study of the use of Enthymemes in the Synoptic Gospels, Persuasive Artistry, Journal for the study of New Testament*, Supplement Series 50, Sheffield Academic Press, Sheffield, England, 1991.

Ward, K (ed.), *Jesus and His Times*, Reader's Digest Association, New York, 1988.

Waruta DW, *Marriage and Family in Contemporary African Society*, in Warutu DW & Kinoti HW, *Pastoral Care in African Christianity*, Action Publishers, Nairobi, 2000.

Washington HC, *The Strange Woman*, in [1] Eskenazi TC & Richards KH, *Second Temple Studies: 2 Temples and Community in the Persian Period*, JSOT Press, Sheffield, England, 1994.

Washington HC, *Wealth and Poverty in the Instruction of Amenemope and the Hebrew Proverbs*, Society of Biblical Literature: Dissertation Series, Scholars Press, Atlanta, (?)

Watson D, Hauser A, *Rhetorical Criticism of the Bible*, EJ Brill, New York, 1994.

Weinberg JP, *Demographische Notizien zur Geschichte der nachexilischen Gemeinde in Juda*, Klio, Volume 54, 1972.

Weller L, Weller TS, *Strange Bedfellows: A Study of Mixed Religious Marriages*, in Liebman CS (ed), *Religious and Secular: Conflict and Accommodation between Jews in Israel*, Keter, Jerusalem, 1990.

Weullner W, *Where is Rhetorical Criticism taking us?* Catholic Biblical Quarterly, Vol. 49. No.3, July, 1987.

Whiston W (Translator), *The Works of Josephus*, Complete and Unabridged, Hendrickson Publishers, Massachusetts, 1987.

Williamson HGM, *Ezra and Nehemiah*, (Old Testament Guides), Sheffield Academic Press, England 1987.

Williamson HGM, *Ezra, Nehemiah*, Waco, Texas, 1985.

Williamson HGM, *The Concept of Israel in Transition*, in Clements RE, *The World of Ancient Israel: Sociological, Anthropological and Political Perspectives*, Cambridge University, Cambridge, (?)

Wolf HW, *Anthropology of the Old Testament*, Fortress Press, Philadelphia, 1974.

Wuellner W, *Reading Romans in context*, Unpublished essay distributed to the SNTS Semina on Reader Response Criticism, 1987.

Yee GA, *The Foreign Women in Proverbs 1-9*, *Journal for the Study of Old Testament*, Volume 43, 1989.

INDEX